THE
SAILING CRUISER
MANUAL

THE SAILING CRUISER MANUAL

John Mellor

DAVID & CHARLES
Newton Abbot   London   North Pomfret (Vt)

For Squiffy

797.124

533117

The following illustrations are reproduced by kind permission:
Hydrographer of the Navy: Figures 71, 73, 74, 78 and 79
Macmillan & Co: Figures 70 and 72
Stanford Maritime: Figures 61, 62, 64 and 65

British Library Cataloguing in Publication Data

Mellor, John, 1945–
    The sailing cruiser manual
    1. Sailing cruisers. Sailing. Seamanship
    – Manuals
    I. Title
    623.88′22

ISBN 0-7153-9274-3

Phototypeset by Typesetters (Birmingham) Ltd,
Smethwick, West Midlands
and printed in Great Britain
by Redwood Burn Limited, Trowbridge
for David & Charles Publishers plc
Brunel House   Newton Abbot   Devon

Published in the United States of America
by David & Charles Inc
North Pomfret   Vermont 05053   USA

Contents

1   The Sailing Life   7
2   Starting to Sail   9
3   The Sails and Rigging   25
4   Manoeuvring Under Sail   39
5   Tides and Anchoring   53
6   Knots and Seamanship   67
7   Life Aboard the Boat   82
8   Weather Forecasting   91
9   Sailing in Strong Winds   103
10 Making a Coastal Passage   111
11 Emergency Routines   130
12 The Auxiliary Engine   138

13 Essential Maintenance   146
14 Buying a Sailing Cruiser   151
15 More Advanced Cruising   161

APPENDICES
1   Equipment Lists   171
2   Electronic Equipment   173
3   Sources of Information   176
4   Useful References   178
5   The RYA Training Scheme   182
Glossary of Nautical Terms   185
Index   189

1

The Sailing Life

For many of us, for many reasons, getting out on the water provides perhaps the truest of all escapes from the pressures of modern life. There is something about water – particularly seawater – that is curiously attractive to we humans. Whether it be the buoyant motion, reminiscent perhaps of life in the womb, or simply the fact that we ourselves are composed mostly of water, or whether it be one or more of a hundred other reasons, I leave to the psychiatrists, the physicians and the philosophers to resolve.

For myself, I think the attraction is a mixture of contentment and challenge. The contentment comes with being in an essentially simple environment in which the simple qualities and pleasures of life become paramount. There is no need to fly out to the Taj Mahal to see a beautiful sunset; they happen all the time at sea. The most dramatic and expensive Marineland can never show you dolphins as you will see them from the deck of a small boat, alone in a seemingly endless expanse of water. The finest and most sophisticated of dinner parties ashore will never give you the pleasure to be had from sharing a simple meal on board with convivial fellow sailors.

Even from a more practical and mundane viewpoint there are considerable benefits to be had from holidaying on your own boat, particularly if you have children. There are no expensive hotel bills to pay; no airport transfers and delays; no constant packing and unpacking, travelling, waiting or queuing. You do not have fixed meal times or prearranged tours to rigidly control your spare time. You can get up in the morning (or the afternoon!) and eat what you like, when you like; then browse through the chart, check the weather forecast, and decide on the spur of the moment where you want to go for the day, and when. And if you do not feel like going anywhere you can simply sit on deck in the sun, or put a fishing line over the side, go swimming, or pack a picnic lunch and row to a quiet nearby beach with the children. Your time is your own, and what you do with it is for you alone to decide. Which makes life afloat a real challenge.

The essential challenge of going to sea in a small sailing cruiser is that you, as the skipper, are on your own. You, and you alone, are totally responsible for the safety and well-being of the vessel and her crew. Out at sea there are no garages, no boatyards, no doctors, dentists, plumbers or what-have-you to ring up in an emergency. There is no corner shop open for

the jar of coffee you forgot and no-one to whom you can pass the buck if things go wrong. The satisfaction to be gained from putting to sea in a sailing boat comes directly from the independence and self-reliance fostered by these challenges. Contentment and relaxation automatically follow when the challenges have been met.

Self-reliance alone, however, is not enough at sea; you need knowledge as well. Much of this can only come from practical experience but this book will give you a thorough grounding in the basics of owning and sailing small cruisers. You will need to build and develop your knowledge through practice and experience, as well as the study of more specialised books, many of which are listed in Appendix 3.

2

Starting to Sail

Let us start at the beginning. What is a sailing boat? In the early days it was simply a boat that was blown along by the pressure of wind on a sheet of canvas or whatever, hung on a mast. Over the years this elementary sail was refined and developed until it was discovered that one could actually sail towards the wind with it. Why this should be possible, we will look at later. For now, let us content ourselves with seeing how we can do so.

In figure 1 we can see an original simple sail above the modern version that you will find on a small sailing cruiser. The mast has changed little in principle, but the old square sail has been split into two and tapered to a point at the top. The sail at the front of the boat is known as the **foresail** (being to the fore) and the one at the back the **mainsail** (because generally it is the most important). You can see in photo 1 that both these sails pivot about their front edges, the mainsail being attached to the mast and the foresail to a wire running from the front of the boat to the top of the mast. Both sails are thus free to flap in the wind. To enable us to control them – pull them towards the wind so that they fill with wind and drive the boat along – we have a rope fastened to the rear corner of each sail which we can pull on to stop them flapping, just as we would a

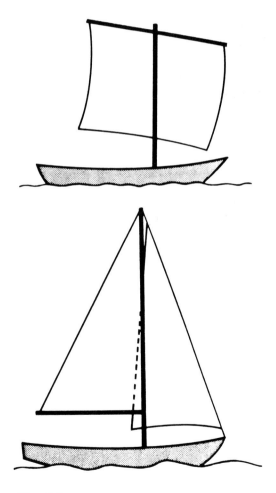

Figure 1

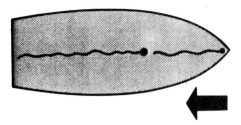

Figure 2

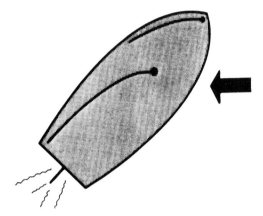

Figure 3

Photo 1

shirt hanging on a washing line. For some reason these controlling ropes are called **sheets.**

In figure 2 we look on the boat from above. We can see that with the wind blowing from right ahead the sails merely flap. Photo 2 shows the boat as the wind would see it. As the sails need to be full of wind to drive the boat it should be apparent that the boat cannot sail directly towards the wind. In figure 3 the wind is blowing from one side of the boat, sufficiently far round that we can haul in on the sheets and fill the sails with wind. Most modern sailing cruisers need the wind to be about 40 to 45° away from the centreline before they can begin sailing. This is the closest to the wind they can sail and it is known as sailing **close-hauled.** Photo 3 shows a small cruiser sailing closehauled with the wind blowing towards it from its righthand side.

You will notice that the foresail is aligned with the mainsail at roughly the same angle to the centreline. This enables it to direct a flow of wind round the **lee side** (opposite the wind) of the mainsail, which increases the latter's efficiency. With both sails hauled in tight to hold the wind, we steer the boat so as to keep the wind roughly 45° off the centreline by watching a small flag at the top of the mast known as a **burgee.** Some boats use a little windvane that they can align with metal rods set at suitable angles to each side of the centreline; the whole assembly being fitted to the top of the mast. And that, in essence, is how a boat sails to **windward** (towards the wind).

As the boat begins to move, two things are likely to become immediately apparent. The first is that the **tiller** (a stick we hold in order to move the rudder, which steers the boat) will tend to pull

Photo 2

Photo 3

over to **leeward** (away from the wind). This action turns the rudder and tries to swing the boat up towards the wind. A firm, steady pressure will be needed on the tiller to counteract this tendency and keep her sailing straight. This inclination of the boat to swing into the wind is known as **weather helm** and is designed into the boat as a safety factor to ensure that, should you let go of the tiller, it will swing into the wind whereupon the sails will flap and stop driving it. See figure 4.

The second thing you will notice, unless the wind is very light, is that the boat will heel over away from the wind, due to the sideways pressure of the wind on the sails. This can be very worrying to the novice, but rest assured the designers know all about it. To counteract this tendency of the wind to blow the boat over, a very heavy weight known as a **keel** is fastened underneath. As the boat heels

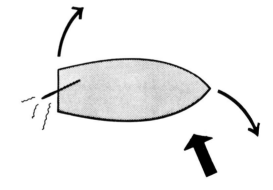

Figure 4

over, so this keel exerts a force to bring it upright again, as you can see in figure 5. The further the boat heels over, the stronger will be this righting force. The heavy part of the keel is fastened at the bottom of the underwater part of the boat, and this underwater section also serves to prevent the wind blowing the boat sideways through the water. See figure 6 and photos 4 and 5.

Having settled down and got the boat sailing steadily closehauled, you will notice that the burgee now lies much closer to the centreline than the 45° we mentioned earlier. This is due to the forward motion of the boat trying to align the burgee with the centreline. The faster the boat goes, the closer to the centreline will the burgee lie. To check whether you are sailing as close to the wind as you can, push the tiller slightly to leeward and allow the boat to swing slowly towards the wind. Watch the front edge of the foresail carefully and you will see it just begin to flap as you get too close to the wind. Pull gently on the tiller then and

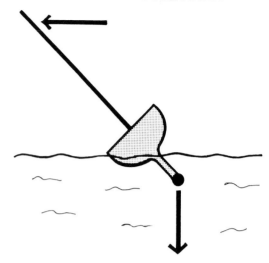

Figure 5

opposite
Photo 4
Photo 5

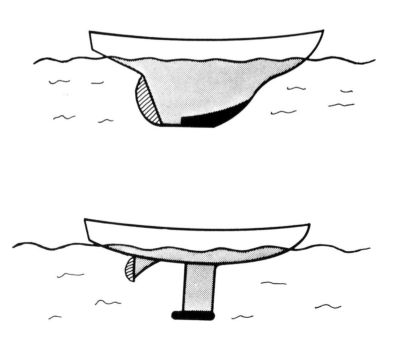

Figure 6

12

Photo 6

Photo 7

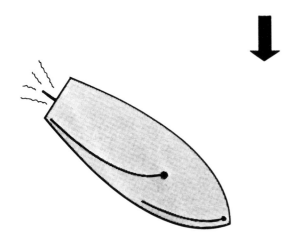

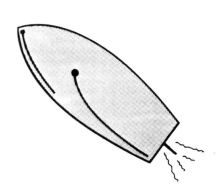

Figure 7

swing the boat slowly away from the wind again until the foresail stops flapping. You should do this all the time you are sailing closehauled – constantly edge her up into the wind until the foresail begins to flap, then swing away again until it stops. You will soon get the hang of it, and learn the normal position for your burgee while sailing closehauled. And that, stripped of the details and mystique, is how we sail a boat closehauled. There is nothing difficult or magical about it.

Sailing closehauled on **starboard tack** (with the wind coming from the righthand side of the boat) is not difficult but it does rather limit the direction in which we can go. However, if we can sail closehauled on starboard tack, then presumably we can also sail just as well with the wind on the lefthand side of the boat, known as **port tack.** And so we can. The process is exactly the same. In figure 7 the left boat is sailing closehauled on port tack and the right one on starboard tack. Photo 6 shows a small cruiser on port tack, while in photo 7 you can see the same boat on starboard tack. Port and starboard are words used to describe the left and right sides of a boat when facing forward.

In figure 8 you can see that by the simple expedient of zig-zagging between port and starboard tacks we can slowly make progress directly towards the wind. The process of changing tacks is known as **tacking** or **going about** and it is a very simple business. All we do is push the tiller to leeward in order to swing the boat towards the wind, then let the swing continue until the wind is about 45° on the other side. As the boat comes head into the wind and the sails flap, the foresail sheet must be let go and the one on the other side hauled in. The mainsail has only one sheet to the centre of the boat, so will swing automatically across and into the right position for the other tack. Note the sheets in photos 6 and 7.

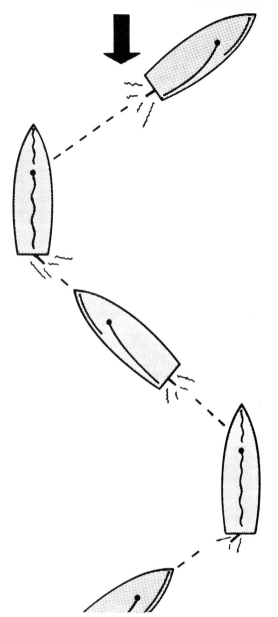

Figure 8

Sailing in directions other than close-hauled requires a slightly different technique. When sailing closehauled we haul the sails in tightly and steer the boat so as to keep as close to the wind as possible. This automatically keeps the sails trimmed correctly all the time. When sailing in any other direction we must reverse all this – steer the boat in the direction we want to go, and trim the sails in until they just stop flapping. Instead of then fixing the sails and constantly adjusting the course to allow for slight changes in wind direction, we fix the course and constantly trim the sails, by letting them out until they begin to flap then hauling them in till they just stop. Sailing in any direction other than closehauled or directly away from the wind is known as reaching, and boats **reaching** on both port and starboard tacks can be seen in figure 9 and photos 8 and 9.

Photo 8

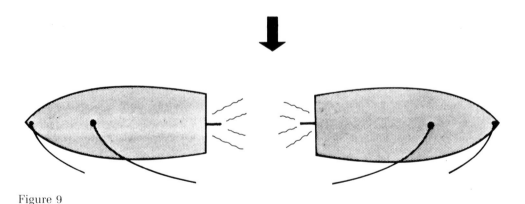

Figure 9

Photo 9

Photo 10

Photo 11

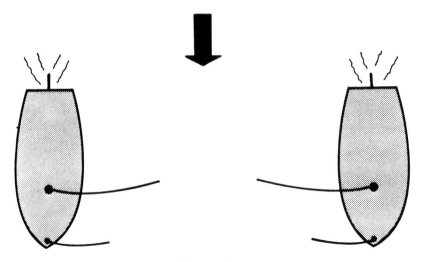

Figure 10

Photo 12

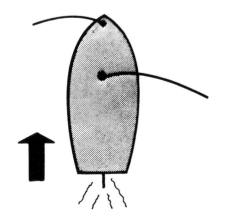

Figure 11

Paradoxically, the most difficult **point of sailing** with modern sails is **running** with the wind right **astern** (behind the boat). With the wind in this direction the sails have to be let out until they are roughly at right angles to the centreline (and the wind). You can see boats running on both port and starboard tacks in figure 10 and photos 10 and 11. It should be apparent from figure 10 that with the wind right astern it does not matter which tack you are on. It should also be noticeable in the photos that the foresail in this situation tends to hang limp, being blanketed from the wind by the larger mainsail. In figure 11 and photo 12 you can see a simple way of solving this problem, by setting the foresail on the opposite side of the boat to the mainsail. This is known as **goosewinging.**

So far no problems. The difficulty with running, especially if the boat is lurching around in a rough sea, is avoiding the wind suddenly getting round the back of the mainsail and blowing onto its lee side. If this happens, the sail, together with the **boom** (the long piece of wood or metal attached to the bottom of the sail) will be blown right across to the other side of the boat. In a strong wind this can happen with sufficient force to kill anyone hit by the boom of a large boat. It can also break booms and masts and tear sails, and cause the boat to swing round very sharply and heel over dramatically. At best it can be embarrassing, at worst extremely dangerous. It is thus most important to watch the burgee very carefully at all times when running, and alter course as necessary to ensure that the wind does not get round behind the mainsail. The boat should be steered to keep the burgee blowing straight ahead along the centreline. See figure 12.

If we control a turn to bring the wind round the back of the mainsail, however, it is perfectly safe in all but the strongest of winds. Swinging the boat round like this is known as **gybing** and the secret is to haul the mainsail tight into the centreline

19

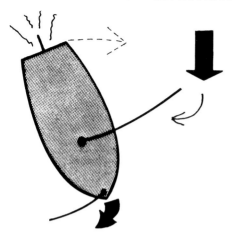

Figure 12 If the wind swings to blow even slightly from the same side as the mainsail, you must immediately alter course as shown to bring the stern towards the wind.

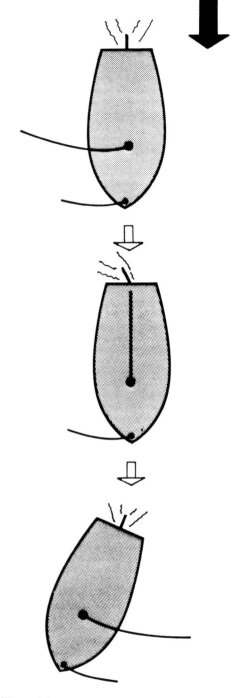

before turning the boat, so that when the wind gets on the other side the boom hardly moves at all, the sail simply flicking across as the wind goes behind it. The mainsheet can then be let out slowly until the boat is running on the other tack. See figure 13. Even when controlled like this the boat will tend to gripe up into the wind as the boom goes over, so you must be prepared to correct this immediately with the tiller.

At this stage it is all too easy to imagine that a sailing boat has three directions in which it can sail – closehauled, reaching, and running. This, of course, is patently nonsense; it can sail anywhere between closehauled on port tack, through the reaching and running positions round to closehauled on starboard tack, by trimming sails as required in order to utilise the force of the wind most efficiently. You can also deliberately trim sails incorrectly in order to slow down, or even stop if they flap completely. This can be an extremely useful way in which to manoeuvre and will be discussed later.

All directions between closehauled and running are referred to generally as reaching, and this point of sailing is loosely

Figure 13

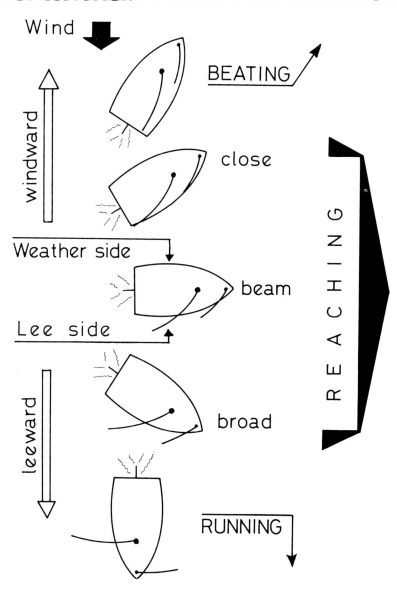

Figure 14a

sub-divided into **beam reaching** (with the wind on the beam – directly from the side of the boat); **close reaching** (between this and closehauled); and **broad reaching** (between a beam reach and a run). These points of sailing can be seen in figures 14a and 14b, together with some basic terminology relating to the boat itself.

And that, in essence, is how to sail a small cruiser. Although I would not decry the magic and mystery that there undoubtedly is in sailing, there are no black arts involved in the basic business of moving a boat through the water using the force of wind on the sails. It is not even necessary to understand the scientific reasons why wind blowing over a sail will push a boat through the water, although it is helpful to visualise the forces and pressures involved. A simple description is given in figure 15.

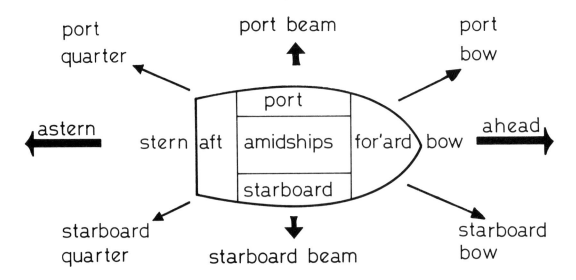

port
quarter

port beam

port
bow

astern

stern | aft | amidships | for'ard | bow

port

amidships

starboard

ahead

starboard
quarter

starboard beam

starboard
bow

Figure 14b

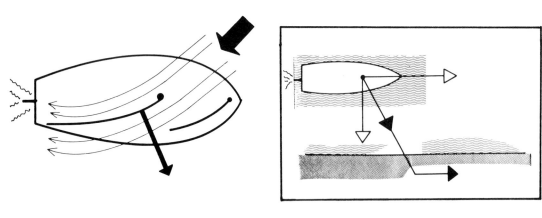

Figure 15 The wind blowing round the lee side of the mainsail has further to travel than that on the weather side, and in order to preserve the status quo it must move faster than the weather side wind. Nothing is free in this world and the increase in speed is paid for by a decrease in pressure. This reduction in pressure on the lee side of the sail creates a suction force acting at right angles to the sail. This force can be resolved by the parallelogram of forces into a forward component and a sideways component. The latter is resisted by the keel, while the former drives the boat along. The action is somewhat similar to the horse towing a barge along a canal, as in the boxed diagram.

Sails and Steering

We mentioned weather helm earlier in the chapter – the way the boat is designed to swing head to wind if the tiller is released. To handle a boat under sail competently it is important to understand what causes this, as it can have major effects on steering and control.

The sideways pressure of the wind on the sails can be said to concentrate its efforts at a single point in the sailplan, known as the **Centre of Effort (CE)**. Equally, the pressure of water on the keel and underwater part of the boat, preventing sideways movement, can also be considered to act at a single point, known as the **Centre of Lateral Resistance (CLR)**. If you lay a pencil on a desk and push on it from each side with fingers directly opposite each other, the pencil will remain still. If you move one finger nearer to an end of the pencil than the other then the pencil will twist. The positioning of

the Centres of Effort and Lateral Resistance in a sailing boat will have the same effects, weather helm being caused by the CE being aft of the CLR, thus tending to swing the boat round into the wind. See figure 16.

The significance of this is that for a boat to steer responsively without careering up into the wind or away from the wind, the sail area must be evenly spread along the boat. If you sheet the jib in tightly and slacken the main right off, then the CE will move forward (there being considerably reduced sideways pressure of wind on the flapping mainsail) and weather helm will decrease, probably to the point where **Lee helm** sets in: the boat will tend to swing away from the wind – a dangerous state of affairs as it will run away downwind out of control if left alone. Conversely, if the CE is too far aft of the CLR (main sheeted in too tight on a reach perhaps), the boat will be heavy to steer as it will be constantly trying to swing

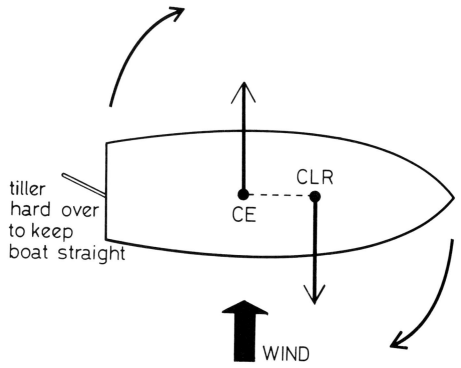

tiller
hard over
to keep
boat straight

CLR

CE

WIND

Figure 16

strongly into the wind.

The real importance of understanding this will become apparent later. For instance, in Chapter 9, when we discuss reducing the size of the sails for strong winds, you will then appreciate that the overall shape of the sailplan needs to be maintained in order to keep the steering balanced. Also, when manoeuvring under sail in restricted spaces the balance of steering is vital; excessive weather helm could prevent the boat swinging away from the wind altogether, while excessive lee helm could prevent you coming up into the wind. Although the residual balance is created by the designed size and shape of the sails and the position of the mast, in relation to the underwater shape of the boat, it can be modified by trimming and adjusting the sails (allowing one to flap completely perhaps, in order to

spill wind pressure from it) in order to move the CE forward or aft as required.

In small boats the CLR can also be moved simply by adjusting the way the boat sits in the water. Moving weights (or even people) forward will immerse the bow, thus putting more resistance in the water forward, which will move the CLR forward and increase weather helm. Think about how CE and CLR can be moved about, and practise trimming sails and boat to see what the real effects are on your boat.

Technically speaking this description of balance is greatly simplified, but it serves perfectly adequately for the practical sailor going about the business of sailing his boat. If you understand this simple picture of sail balance, you will have no trouble trimming your boat so that it will steer and handle properly.

3

The Sails and Rigging

Before the boat can be sailed as described in the last chapter its sails must of course be hoisted and the means of controlling them understood.

In photos 13 and 14 we see a small cruiser without sails set and the same one with mainsail and foresail hoisted. The most common type of foresail is known as a **jib.** Let us deal first with the hoisting and control of the mainsail.

Photo 13

Photo 14

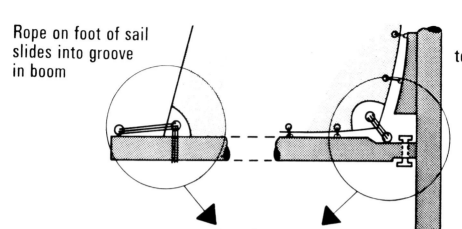

Rope on foot of sail slides into groove in boom

Sliders tied to sail run in tracks on boom and mast

See photographs

Figure 17 The sail can be attached either by sliders tied to it that run in tracks on mast and boom, or by ropes sewn to the edges that run inside grooves in mast and boom.

The boom, to which the **foot** of the sail is attached, is fixed permanently to the mast at a suitable height to keep the sail as low as possible (so reducing the heeling force of the wind) without knocking our heads off. The fitting – a sort of universal joint allowing the boom to swivel – is called a **gooseneck.** The foot of the sail is fastened to the top of the boom in various ways, the two most commonly used being shown in figure 17. The two lower corners of the sail are fixed separately by means of metal or plastic eyelets fitted into the sail. The front corner, known as the **tack,** is fastened to the gooseneck fitting, and the rear corner – the **clew** – is lashed to an eye in the end of the boom, and also round the boom itself in order to spread the load. See figure 17 and photos 15 and 16. The clew lashing is often called an **outhaul,** as it hauls the sail out along the boom, and

sometimes it is adjustable while sailing for purposes of fine tuning to different wind conditions. Details will vary.

The sail is generally attached to the mast in a similar way as to the boom, and is hoisted by a rope or wire called a **halyard** fastened to the top corner of the sail (the **head**). The halyard goes round a sheave at the masthead and down (inside or outside the mast) to a **cleat** near the foot of the mast to which it is secured. Precise details vary; some boats having winches to assist as it is important that the **luff** of the sail (front edge) is hoisted as tightly as possible. Often the gooseneck slides on a track and a small tackle (pronounced 'taykel' on boats) is used to haul it down tight after hoisting the sail. This is known as a **tack tackle**, as it hauls down the tack of the sail as another way of achieving a tight luff. They are sometimes found also on jibs. **Battens** (stiff lengths of wood or plastic) will be found fitted into pockets in the **leech** of the sail (rear edge), to help it keep shape and also prevent it flogging too much.

Photo 15

Photo 16

Setting the Sails

Before hoisting the mainsail, make sure first that the mainsheet is slack so that the sail can swing freely in the wind. Many boats have a **boom vang** rigged from the boom to the bottom of the mast in order to stop the former from lifting high into the air when gybing and so on. This should be fitted and hauled tight after the mainsail is rigged. See the tackle in photo 17, and also the black halyard cleats on the mast. Fit battens, slacken mainsheet, hoist halyard tightly and cleat as shown in figure 18; haul down on tack tackle then boom vang, and the boat should look like the one in photo 18. Remember that the boat must be pointing **head to wind** before hoisting the mainsail or the sail will fill with wind and start her sailing embarrassingly round her **mooring**.

Now let us set the jib. Because this sail is free to swing right round and flap

Photo 17

whatever the wind direction, it can be hoisted in any wind direction. The mechanics of hoisting and setting are just the same as for the mainsail except that there is (apart from a few exceptions) no boom. The tack is attached to a fitting at the **bow** (front of the boat), the luff fixed to the **forestay** (wire from bow to masthead) using various types of clip (usually known as **jib hanks**); the sheets (one leading to each side of the boat) secured to the clew and the sail hoisted on a halyard. Some modern boats have a system in which the jib is permanently rigged to a special forestay and is rolled tightly round it when finished with. This saves a lot of effort but can cause problems as we will mention later. Methods vary, but in principle the sail is furled by pulling on a line that winds a drum at the bottom of the forestay, and is set by loosening this line and hauling out on the sheets. They are known as **roller-furling** jibs. See photo 19. Increasingly, mainsails are also being fitted in a similar fashion, rolling up

inside the mast itself or round a special gadget attached to the after side of the mast. The control lines for these systems are often led to the **cockpit** (the place where you sit and steer) so that sails can be set or furled without having to go on deck.

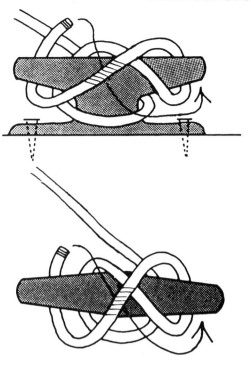

Photo 18

Figure 18 Take half a turn round the stem of the cleat then continue turning round the horns in figures of eight until the cleat is full of rope. Finish off by twisting the last turn over the top horn so that the end is tucked under the turn for security. Cleats should be angled so that the halyards lead directly to the bottom of the stem for the first turn. It matters not whether a halyard is turned up clockwise or anticlockwise, but it must go to the bottom first or the loaded halyard will be jammed behind the turns, which can cause problems when you try to ease the halyards smoothly round the cleat to lower the sail. This point is most important when anything under strain is cleated, be it halyard, sheet, mooring warp or whatever.

Photo 19

Main and Jib Sheets

The basic layout of the sheets can be seen in figure 19, and this should be compared with the real thing in photo 14. The mainsail can be difficult to haul in when the wind is blowing, so the mainsheet usually incorporates a tackle with a purchase of something like four to one, thus enabling us to haul it in with a quarter of the effort. One end is attached to the boom and the other to a strong point usually at the **stern** (back end) of the boat, although sometimes it comes down ahead of the cockpit. See photo 18. The hauling part is normally led to a cleat to which it is secured. In small boats this may be replaced by a **jamming cleat** on the bottom block, as you can see at the bottom of the boom vang in photo 17. The rope is automatically gripped as you pull it through this and is released by a sharp downward jerk to free it from the jaws.

The jibsheet is in two parts so that one can be used on either side of the boat. Each part is led through a **fairlead** or block (the former being a smooth wood or plastic eye) to a cleat at the side of the cockpit, a winch usually being available to haul it tight. When tacking or gybing the mainsheet looks after itself, but the jibsheet taking the weight must be let go slack and the one on the other side hauled in as the boat goes round. The jib is sheeted in on the **leeward** side of the boat (opposite the wind) and the **windward** sheet must be kept slack so as not to pull on the clew of the jib and distort its shape. See figure 19. Special knots called **figure of eight knots** are tied in the ends of all sheets to prevent them from accidentally running out through the blocks or fairleads when let go. See figure 20 and photo 20. These should be far enough from the end of the sheet that if they pull up tight against a fairlead there is enough end to grip firmly and haul on. The jibsheet fairleads are normally movable fore and

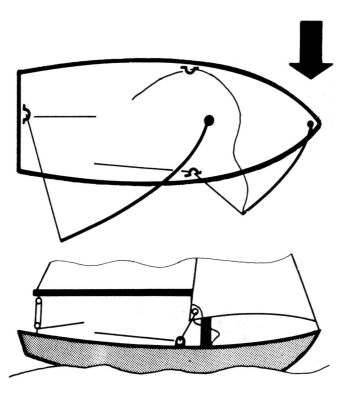

Figure 19

aft and can be set so that the sheets produce the best angle of pull on the clew of the jib. This is when the strain is evenly spread between the foot and leech of the sail. If the leech flaps and the foot is tight, the fairlead needs to go further forward so that the sheet pulls downwards more and tightens the leech. If the foot flaps, the fairlead must go further aft in order to tighten it.

Working the Winches

The winch in photo 20 is worked by simply wrapping three turns of the sheet round it and winching back and forth on the handle while hauling on the sheet. Although designs vary (some have handles on the top that are wound round and round; some have two speeds; some are **self-tailing** in that they grip the sheet as you wind so that you do not have to haul on it) the principle remains the same. In strong winds winches need to be used with care as they can easily trap fingers with considerable force, and if turns of the sheet are allowed to ride over one another the whole lot can jam solid, making it impossible to release the sheet. The dangers in this should be apparent.

The general principle of working a winch is to put just one or two turns on at first (check which way round the winch rotates before putting them on!) and haul in as fast as possible until the weight of wind begins to come on the sheet. Then carefully wind on further turns to a total of three or four (depending on wind strength), keeping firm hold of the weight while doing so and your hand well clear of the winch in case you get suddenly pulled towards it. Make quite certain the turns are cleanly on the barrel and not riding over one another, then wind in on the handle while leaning back on the sheet so that your weight helps to hold it and the chance of being overbalanced is reduced. Then turn the sheet up round the cleat perhaps four or five times to ensure that it grips securely. This is much easier and safer with two people – one winching and the other **tailing** (hauling on the sheet). Winch handling is discussed in more detail in Chapter 6.

Photo 20

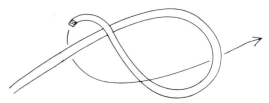

Figure 20

Handing and Stowing the Sails

Removing the sails (**handing** sails as it is known) is simply the reverse of setting them. The mainsail is normally left on mast and boom and lashed securely to the boom using short ties of rope or elastic as you can see in photo 21. See also photo 13 for a neat stow. The sail should be hauled **aft** (towards the stern) along the boom to spread it evenly, then furled as tightly and

lashed as securely as possible to prevent the wind blowing it all apart. With the sail down the boom needs to be held up by something and a **topping lift** is generally used. In figure 21 you can see two types – one is like a halyard from the top of the mast to the end of the boom and can be hauled on to take the weight of the boom before lowering the mainsail, and the other is a short line from the **backstay** (wire from top of mast to stern) which

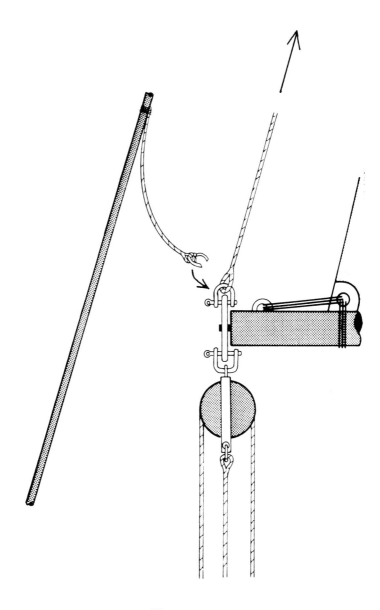

Figure 21

Photo 21

simply clips onto the boom end to hold it up after the sail has been handed.

Handing the jib is slightly different as it is normally removed completely and stowed below in a bag. Having lowered it on the halyard, the sail should be un-clipped from the forestay starting at the head. As the sail comes free of the stay so it should be steadily stuffed into its bag, the head going in first. If you are handing the sail at sea in any wind this enables you to keep it under control without it blowing away. As you near the foot of the sail the sheets should be unfastened and the clew stuffed in the bag so that the tack finally goes in last. This means that when setting the sail you can hold the bag firmly between your knees and get the tack out and attached to the stemhead first. The clew comes next, to be secured to the sheets, then the rest of the sail can be hauled out bit by bit and clipped to the forestay as it comes. The sail is thus completely under control all the time and cannot blow away. Also, it is very easy to hoist a jib upside down unless the corners are clearly labelled, and knowing that the tack is always at the top of the bag avoids this embarrassment.

In photo 13 you can see a small cruiser on her mooring with sails down and everything neatly and firmly stowed. It is quite incredible the power of a strong wind to pull apart furled sails, so this neatness has a purpose other than mere smart appearance. You can see how tightly the mainsail is furled and lashed. The boom is held securely on the topping lift and prevented from flying about by hauling down tightly on the mainsheet. The jibsheets are fastened to the forestay, and hauled tight onto their cleats, and, if you look carefully, you can see short lines tied from the **shrouds** (wires from mast-head to each side of the boat) to the halyards to pull them clear of the mast. They are known as **frapping lines** and without them the halyards will bang and rattle incessantly against the mast. If the mast is varnished wood the varnish will be hacked off in no time by this, and if it is aluminium (usual in modern boats) the noise this makes will drive everyone nearby totally insane! Lengths of elastic shockcord with hooks on the end are often used. Furling jibs theoretically need only rolling up with the furling line. In practice they can come unfurled in strong winds, so a secure lashing should be put round them where the sheets lead out.

Whether the sails are set or stowed there will be long lengths of halyards lying about on the deck. If they are left there they will soon fall over the side and generally get tangled in everything and everybody, so we must stow them tidily. There are two basic ways of doing this, having first coiled the halyard close to the cleat as shown in photo 22. All ropes on a boat should be coiled in a clockwise direction, as seen here, because they will lie more naturally that way. NEVER coil

Photo 22

them rcund hand and elbow, as often seen on nautical TV soap operas! The resulting coil will bear a close resemblance to a nest of writhing grass snakes. If the rope tries to twist as you coil it, then gently untwist it until it lies naturally in the coil. We can then simply wedge the coil between the halyard and the mast, just above the cleat, or (if the coil is large) we can pull the end leading from the cleat through the centre of the coil, give it a twist or two, then hook the eye that is formed over the top of the cleat, thus enabling the coil to hang cleanly from the cleat. See photo 23. The coil should be held close to the cleat while doing this, so that it is firmly gripped against it by the twisted eye.

When the halyards are required – for setting or handing the sails – the coil should be released from its stowage and dropped onto the deck so that the part leading up to the cleat lies on top. This is particularly important when handing sails as it allows the halyard to run out from the top of the coil as the sail is lowered, without tangling.

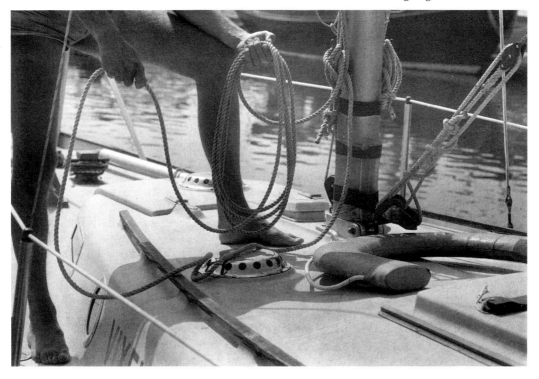

Photo 23

The Mast and Rigging

In figure 22 you can see the basic wires that generally hold up a mast. As usual designs vary, but this should give you a good idea of what to expect. In essence a backstay prevents the mast from falling forward, a forestay stops it falling backwards, and shrouds on either side stop it falling sideways. Some boats do not have backstays (a large mainsail getting in the way, perhaps) and their shrouds will lead aft in order to stop the mast falling forward. Larger boats may have **cap-shrouds** to the masthead, held out by poles called **spreaders** in order to improve the angle at which they pull on the mast. Lower shrouds may also be rigged to the mast just below the spreaders. Smaller boats may have less rigging than this.

In practice things are rather less simple than this. Complex and considerable strains are generated in mast and rigging when a boat is sailing and the setting up of a mast and the tensioning of the rigging is a skilled art. Fortunately it is one of those arts that sailors pride themselves on and local experts will fall over themselves to demonstrate their prowess if you ask them to 'tune' your rig! Do check, however, that they are experts. If you are on your own you will not go far wrong if you set the mast to rake very slightly back from the vertical and tighten up the rigging, with the adjustable rigging screws fitted at the bottom, until it plucks with a fairly low, resonant twang. Make sure it does not lean to one side. If you then find the boat has lee helm or excessive weather helm, the CE of the sails can be moved by altering the rake of the mast. Raking it aft will move the sails (and thus their CE) aft and increase weather helm, while raking it forward will reduce weather helm.

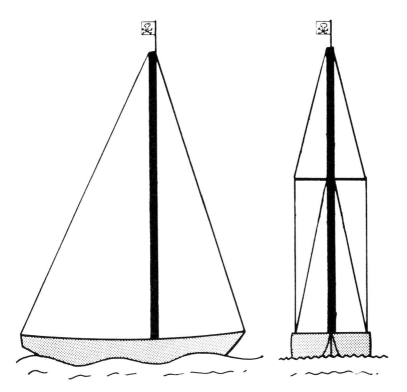

Figure 22

Ancillary Sails

Besides the two basic sails we have discussed – mainsail and jib – most small sailing cruisers will carry extra sails for specific purposes. As we shall see in Chapter 9, when the wind is very strong we must reduce the area of sail that the wind is pressing on. The mainsail is usually reduced in size in situ while the jib is more often changed for a smaller one. The largest jib is referred to as the **Number 1**, and you will likely have a smaller **Number 2**, even smaller **Number 3** and perhaps a very small, extra strong **storm jib**. Certain types of roller furling jibs can simply be rolled up round the forestay and made smaller as the wind freshens, thus saving the necessity for carrying smaller jibs, and the effort of changing to them. A large type of jib that

reaches well back behind the mast is known as a **genoa** and is commonly used on racing boats. It can be a nuisance when cruising as the clew often has to be hauled forward round the mast when tacking. A **spinnaker** is a very large bulbous sail that is set flying from the masthead when running or broad reaching. It increases the speed of a boat tremendously, but can be difficult to handle in any breeze of wind. A compromise for the cruising boat is a sort of cross between a genoa and a spinnaker called a **cruising chute**, which is much easier to handle than a proper spinnaker. These large sails are unsuitable for beginners, and details of handling them will be found in Chapter 15.

Different Rigs

The type of rig that we have discussed so far – with one mast and two triangular sails – is the commonest in small boats and is called a **bermudan sloop**. The bermudan mainsail is triangular and the sloop has one mast with a mainsail and a jib. There are many other types of rig and sail shape, some of which can be found in small modern sailing cruisers but which require some experience to handle. Some of these are described in Chapter 15.

4

Manoeuvring Under Sail

The most important single fact to bear in mind when handling and manoeuvring a boat is that she almost never proceeds in the direction she is pointing. There are two basic reasons for this – one is **leeway** (sideways drift caused by the wind) and the other is **tidal stream** (movement of water caused by the **tides**).

Leeway

This, as mentioned briefly in Chapter 2, is largely prevented by the sideways resistance of the keel. Unless running directly before the wind, however (when drift is in the same direction as travel), there is always a certain amount, depending on area of keel, windage of cabins and masts etc, and the point of sailing.

In general we can say that the greater the keel and underwater area (presenting resistance to the water) the less leeway a boat will make; and the greater the area of boat, cabin top, masts, rigging and so on (presenting resistance to the wind) the more leeway a boat will make. We can also say that the closer to the wind the boat is sailing, the greater will be the leeway. When running before the wind there will be no leeway at all, as the wind pressure is not from the side of the boat. There will be very slight leeway when

reaching with the wind abaft the beam (wind pressure being reduced by the boat sailing away from it), and this will steadily increase as the boat sails closer to the wind, reaching a maximum when she is closehauled (when the wind pressure is increased by the boat sailing towards it).

In figure 23 we can see the exaggerated effect of leeway on a boat sailing closehauled on starboard tack. Although she is pointing in the direction of the solid arrow she actually moves through the water along the line of the pecked arrow. This, as you can imagine, tends to make life rather difficult at times, but there is a simple way to assess the precise direction the boat is moving in when she is making leeway. In figure 24 we see the same boat drifting at an angle towards another small boat that is tied to a mooring and stationary. It should be apparent from the diagram that if we remain in the same part of the boat (at the tiller, say) and line up some object on the boat (mast, shroud or whatever) with the little boat on the mooring, the two will remain in line if we are drifting directly towards her. If our movement will take us ahead of her then the object we have lined up with her will move towards her bow. If we are going to pass astern of her, the object will move steadily towards her stern. This method is

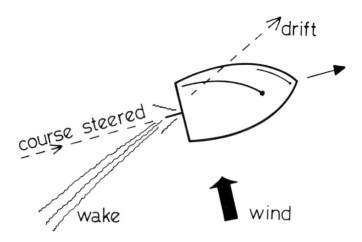

Figure 23

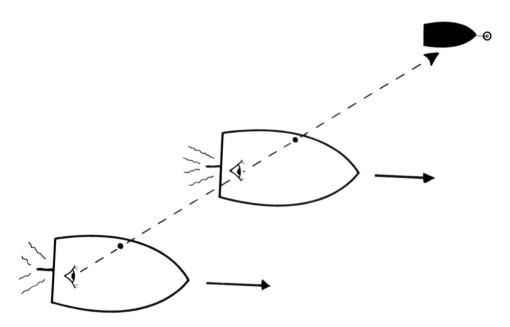

Figure 24

a bit rough and ready but it works well enough; it needs some practice to gauge how rapidly the object has to move to indicate that we will pass clear with a good safety margin. You will also note from figure 23 that the angle of the wake gives some indication of the amount of leeway.

Tidal Stream

Tides are discussed in detail in Chapter 5. For now let us accept that they are movements of water in the sea, caused by the gravitational pull of the moon and the sun. As the positions of sun and moon vary so do the direction and speed of this water flow (the tidal stream) vary. Roughly speaking, the tide rises for about six hours, then falls for six hours, the

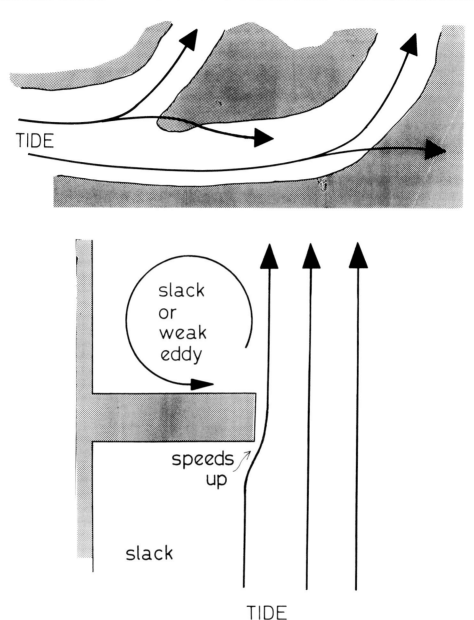

Figure 25 Tidal streams follow the line of least resistance and are generally strongest in the middle of a deep channel, where there is nothing to hinder them. Close to the banks they are slowed considerably by friction against the land and will be almost slack, even occasionally forming back eddies. Friction against the bottom in shallow water also slows down the stream. When the stream is bent, round an obstruction or a bend in a channel, it speeds up on the outside as it has further to travel; and it speeds up through narrow gaps in order to shift all that water through a small space. It will also tend to drift across into bays and side channels – a cross-set that must be guarded against when proceeding along the main channel.

41

highest point being known as **High Water** and the lowest as **Low Water**. As the tide rises it flows up the beaches, into the harbours and estuaries, and is said to be **flooding**. This is the **flood tide**. Six hours later, roughly, it reaches High Water, pauses for a short while, then falls for six hours, during which time it is said to be **ebbing**, as it flows out of the harbours and so on. This is the **ebb tide**. The problem when manoeuvring, is to allow for the way these tidal streams carry us back and forth as they run in and out – as they flood and ebb.

The speeds of tidal streams vary tremendously, depending on the place and circumstances – anything from zero to a speed of ten **knots** or more (a knot is a nautical mile per hour and a nautical mile is about 2000 yards, slightly longer than a land mile). A likely average for a tidal stream is around two or three knots when it is running at its strongest, half-way between High and Low Water. Clearly tidal streams can have more influence on boat-handling than leeway, being often much stronger and also from varying directions. The strength and direction is also more difficult to assess, although the principle of lining up part of the boat with a stationary object in order to note the drift still applies.

Assessing the Tidal Stream

Information on times and heights of tides, and speeds and directions of tidal streams, can be found in certain publications, details of which will be discussed in Chapters 5 and 10. The published speeds and directions of tidal streams are,

Photo 24

Photo 25

however, greatly affected by such things as depth of water, shape of coastlines and so on, and we must learn how to assess the stream with our eyes. Figure 25 shows how streams can be affected by the lay of the land, and we can check these details by observing the flow of water past **buoys**, moored boats, piers and so on. See photos 24 and 25. We can also do so by lining up part of the boat with a stationary object (as for checking leeway) and watching which way the boat is being carried away from the direction she is pointing.

Allowing for Tidal Stream

In the simplest situation, if the stream is running directly against us at two knots, it will slow us down by that amount. Think of the tidal stream as water moving en masse rather like a conveyor belt. If it is running directly with us at three knots it will increase our speed over the ground by that amount. It is important to distinguish here between speed through the

water and speed over the ground. In the first example we may be sailing through the water at two knots, but our speed over the ground (with two knots of tide against us) will be zero. Although we will be getting nowhere we will have two knots of water flowing past the rudder, so enabling us to steer the boat. The significance of this is that while **stemming the tide** we maintain control over the boat, and can steer her sideways across the stream towards a mooring or jetty that we want to tie up to. If the tide is with us, however, there is nothing we can do to prevent it pushing us forwards at its speed plus our own, and the result is that we have little control over the movement of the boat. Thus all manoeuvres to pick up buoys or get alongside jetties and so on should always be conducted stemming the tide, in order to have maximum control over the movement of the boat.

There are two basic ways of gauging speed and direction of movement over the ground, whether the tide is with us, against us, or across the direction being steered. Both will automatically take into account leeway as well. The first is that described in the section on leeway, and the second can be seen in figure 26. If we are sailing in the direction of the thin solid arrow and the tidal stream is running as shown by the thick arrow, the boat will actually move along the line of the pecked arrow. It should be apparent that if two objects ashore are in line along this arrow, they will remain in line so long as we continue moving crabwise along the pecked arrow towards them. Conversely, if we steer so as to maintain the two objects in line, we will move along the pecked arrow towards them. This, in principle, is how we move the boat in the direction we want to go, when under the influence of tidal stream.

The technique for maintaining this controlled sideways movement can be seen in figure 27. You can see that, if the boat drifts to the left of the required line, the object at the back of the pair will appear to

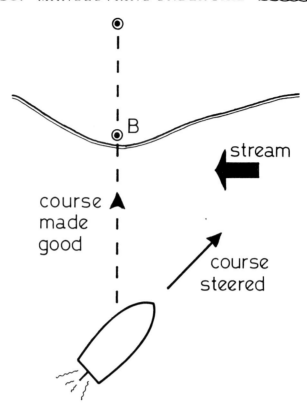

course made good

stream

course steered

B

Figure 26

move to the left of the one at the front. If the boat drifts to the right of the track the rear object will likewise move to the right. To maintain the line, course should be altered boldly towards the front object until they are back in line, then the original course steered again, but with a slight correction to allow for the drift that was experienced. With a little practice you will find that the track can be held by constant slight alterations of course every time the two objects begin to open up. If you do the same thing by keeping a single stationary object in line with part of the boat, you will find that course must be altered towards the far stationary object whenever the boat drifts off the track. If, however, the latter technique is being used to check whether you are drifting onto rocks, a moored boat or anything else that you want actually to avoid, then course must be altered to make the boat move steadily away from the object you wish to avoid, towards the side of it that you want to sail past. Exactly the same principle applies if you wish to avoid a moving object such as another boat. If it remains in line with a part of your boat then the two of you will collide, and you will have to do something to avoid this. There are rules concerning action that should be taken when a likelihood of collision with another vessel exists, and details are given at the end of this chapter.

Even the basic business of simply sailing about involves a fair amount of concentration as we trim sails, set courses to allow for leeway and tidal stream, and keep clear of dangers such as buoys, rocks and other boats. With experience all this will become almost second nature, but it is the most fundamental part of sailing a boat and must be thoroughly learned and practised.

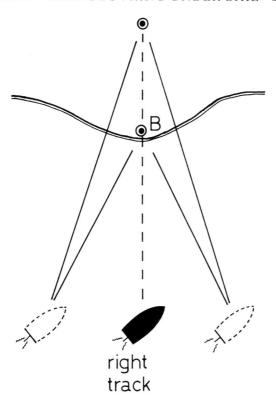

right
track

Figure 27

Leaving a Mooring

Although most boats these days are, for convenience, kept in **marinas** (special harbours for yachts), the techniques involved in leaving and picking up mooring buoys are a most essential part of handling a boat under sail, so we will discuss them first.

Before letting go of a mooring and sailing away we must consider carefully the effects on the boat of wind and tide, both while on the mooring and during those critical moments after first **casting off**. As mentioned above, the direction in which the boat will lie on the mooring depends mainly on the strength and direction of the tidal stream (generally referred to simply as the tide). It is rare that a sailing boat will lie pointing into the wind unless the tide is very weak. The effect of a strong wind is generally to cause her to lie slightly across the tide or, if it is from astern, to sail forward over the buoy, still pointing into the tide. Thus, as we saw in Chapter 3, we need to think carefully about setting the sails while still on the mooring, or we might begin sailing before we have let go. Equally we do not want to let go of the mooring and start drifting about with no sails to control the boat.

What we must do is set the sails in such a way that they will flap freely without driving the boat. We can then let go of the mooring, trim the sails, and sail off immediately with the boat under control. If the wind is blowing from the same direction as the tide (from ahead or nearly ahead), we can simply hoist both sails and they will flap freely in line with the wind. Make sure all sheets are free to run out as the sails flap or they will catch some wind and start the boat sailing all over the place around the mooring. Having decided which way to sail off, and checked that no passing boats or nearby moorings are in the way, simply haul the jib in on the opposite side to the way you want to go until the back of it fills with wind, and then cast off the mooring. See figure 28. This is known as **backing the jib** and is a handy way of moving the bow to one side. As soon as the bow is pointing in the right direction, trim the sails properly and sail away. If this direction is away from the wind make sure the mainsheet is free to run out so the boom and sail can swing right away from the boat. If they stay pinned in tight she may not swing away from the wind, even with the jib backed, as the mainsail will tend to push her bow round into the wind all the time.

If the wind is from astern it will not be possible to set the mainsail as it will fill with wind immediately and start driving the boat around the mooring. In these circumstances, set the jib only, ensuring that both sheets are free to run out so that the sail can blow ahead of the boat. See figure 29. Then unlash the mainsail and get it ready for hoisting before letting go the mooring. With the jib still flapping allow the tide to carry the boat clear of the buoy, then haul in the jib sheet and get the boat moving. With a good speed on and when you are clear of other vessels, round up into the wind and set the mainsail. See figure 29. This needs to be done fairly quickly so you can trim sails and move off before the boat stops and the bow blows away from the wind. If she does stop, the jib can be backed to blow the bow round in the desired direction, as explained in the last paragraph.

With the wind on the beam and the tide

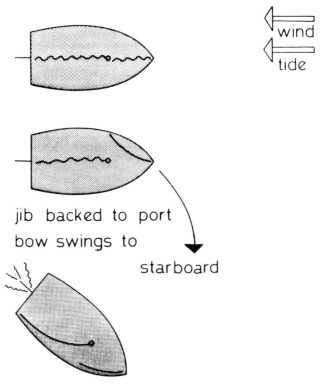

jib backed to port

bow swings to

starboard

boat sails off on port tack

Figure 28

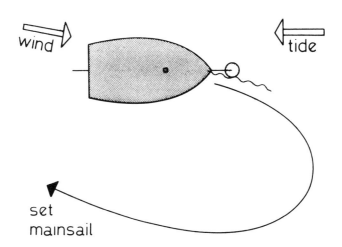

Figure 29

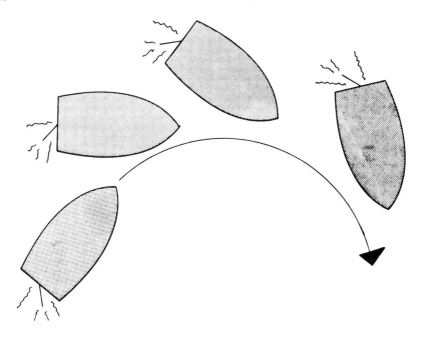

Figure 30

ahead one might think the mainsail could be set before leaving the mooring. In practice, constant shifting of the wind direction and swinging of the boat will inevitably cause it to fill with wind, even if only intermittently, and trouble will ensue. Treat this situation as for a wind from astern as in figure 29. When casting off under jib, remember that few boats will sail to windward properly without the mainsail, so round up and set it as soon as you have enough room, and enough speed to carry you all the way round into the wind. Whatever the wind and tide combination, these are the two basic techniques for getting away from a mooring, and you will have to decide which is the most suitable for the circumstances. There must, however, be no risk of the sails filling with wind before you get away, or you will find yourself in all sorts of trouble. Take your time. Look over the side and at the other moored boats to check the strength and direction of the tide. Think about the strength and direction of the wind. Check carefully for obstructions and work out which way to swing and where you are going to round up and set the mainsail. Make sure the crew know what you will expect of them, and leave when you are ready, not before. Appreciate that when you swing round, the boat will slide through the water away from the turn, as in figure 30, so allow room for such manoeuvres.

Picking up a Mooring

There are two basic things we must do when returning to a mooring. We must arrive and stop close enough to the buoy to lean over the bow and tie up to it; and we must do so with no sails set that might fill with wind and drive us round the buoy. In order to achieve the first it is necessary to reach the buoy pointing in the same direction the boat will lie in after

tying up to it. Unless the tide is slack this will almost certainly be pointing into the tide, which at the same time will then help to slow down and stop the boat. Check from the way other nearby boats are lying, and from the stream running past the buoys, and from your knowledge of whether the tide is ebbing or flooding, which way the stream will be running at the mooring. Do not be afraid to sail slowly past the mooring for a good look before making the final approach to pick it up.

Having decided how you will lie on arrival, work out which sails can safely be left up when secured, checking the relation of wind direction to the direction in which you will lie. See earlier section on leaving a mooring. If wind and tide are together, simply sail closehauled up towards the buoy and swing into the wind at the last minute, gauging the moment which will allow the boat to coast up to a stop head-to-wind at the buoy. The sails can be left set and the sheets slackened off, as you can see in figure 31. Judging the right position from which to luff up head-to-wind and continue just as far as the buoy takes some experience, so practise it.

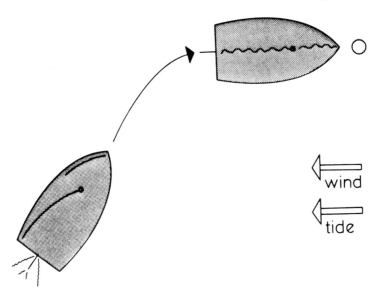

Figure 31

Many skippers prefer to approach on a close reach heading directly for the buoy (allowing for the set of the tide) as this enables them to control their speed of approach accurately by trimming the sails in and out; the sails being allowed to flap freely to stop, on arrival at the buoy.

With wind and tide in opposition, the judgement is rather easier. We know we must approach into the tide (partly to help us slow down and stop, and partly because that is almost certainly how we will lie after tying up), so we must approach the buoy downwind with only the jib set (as the mainsail will not flap freely in this position). This means sailing slowly towards the buoy in a straight line downwind, allowing the jib to flap freely to slow down, and hauling it in again if more way is needed to reach the buoy. On arrival the jib should be dropped on deck immediately you are certain of reaching the buoy, or the sheets will flap around and catch in things, as well as clouting the heads of crew on the foredeck. In strong winds this can be dangerous. See figure 32. With winds across the tide, remember

the drill for slipping from a mooring – if in doubt about whether the mainsail will flap freely, do not set it. Approach as for wind against tide. Take your time and think out carefully how the boat will behave. Look at nearby moored boats; make a dummy run past the mooring if you are uncertain; then make your approach.

Berthing Alongside a Jetty

Although the principles of sail handling and approaching into the tide and so on are just as for leaving and approaching a mooring, there is a big and important difference in this manoeuvre. There is no room on the jetty side for the boat to swing, the sails to flap, or for you to sail away and try again if you get it wrong. Thus rather more skill and experience are required for berthing alongside under sail. Until you gain this, it will be wise to berth alongside jetties, walls, marina pontoons and so on using your auxiliary engine. See Chapter 12. However, here are the basic details of how to do so under sail.

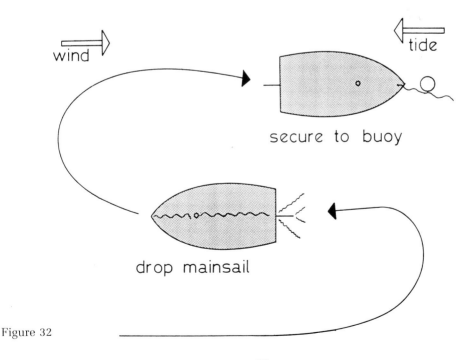

secure to buoy

drop mainsail

Figure 32

With a tide running along the wall (which it generally does) we can see in figures 33a and 33b that the basic techniques for getting alongside with wind and tide together, and with wind and tide opposed, are the same as for picking up a mooring. The difference, as mentioned above, is that a great deal more skill and judgement are required, especially if there are other boats on the wall and you have to fit in between them. Marina berths are likely to be even more difficult as they tend to be packed in closely together (see photo 51 in Chapter 14), and the approach will be extremely constricted. It is advisable to have a crew member standing by with a line at the stern so that if necessary he or she can jump ashore and slow the boat down with it. The line should lead from just for'ard of the cockpit rather than right aft, or the stern will be yanked hard into the wall as she slows. There will be more on the business of tying up alongside in Chapter 6.

Berthing alongside under sail is even more tricky if the wind is across the tide. In figure 34 we see the technique for coping with a wind blowing off the wall. The secret here is to get the bow close enough to the jetty that a crewman can jump ashore with a line and the boat be tied up before she blows away. In figure 35 the wind is blowing onto the jetty and the approach must be made with jib only, handing the sail before reaching the wall in case it snags on anything. The boat should be aimed to stop just clear of the wall to allow for the wind blowing her down onto it, but not so far off that she builds up speed drifting. In all these manoeuvres you must always approach into the tide so that it will slow you down and stop you, and also so that water flow is maintained over the rudder to give steering control.

Leaving an alongside berth is relatively simple unless the wind is blowing onto the berth. If the wind is ahead we can set

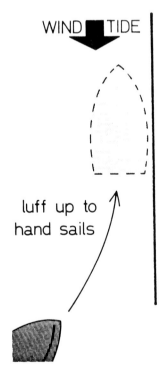

Figure 33a

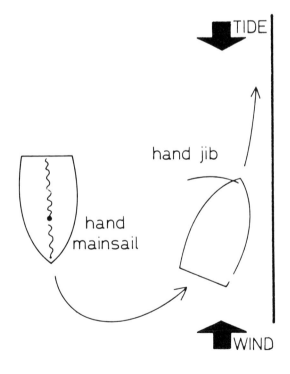

Figure 33b

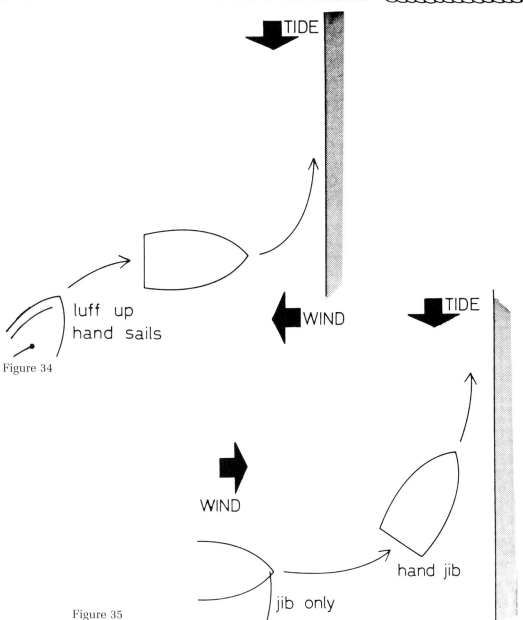

TIDE

WIND

luff up
hand sails

Figure 34

TIDE

WIND

hand jib

jib only

Figure 35

both sails, back the jib to blow the bow clear, then trim the sails and sail away. If the wind is blowing us off the berth we can simply set the jib, cast off the mooring lines and allow it to do so, setting the mainsail and sailing away when the boat is clear enough to luff into the wind a bit while the mainsail is set. If the wind is blowing onto the jetty we must run a line out to some point opposite the jetty and haul the boat off until she is far enough clear to set sail and sail off without drifting back onto the wall. Remember that leeway will be at a maximum when

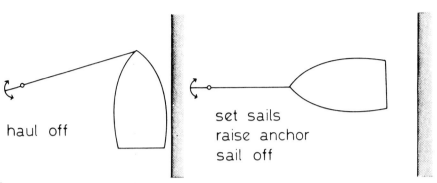

haul off

set sails
raise anchor
sail off

Figure 36

the boat first starts moving slowly off. The other alternative is to row out the anchor on a very long line and haul off on that. See figure 36. The anchor must be far enough out that when the boat is sufficiently clear of the wall to sail away, there is still enough length of anchor rope out to hold her. See Chapter 5 for full information on anchoring.

Rule of the Road

The sea has its own version of the Highway Code, colloquially known as the Rules of the Road, which dictate what vessels should do to avoid colliding with one another. The full rules are complex and contain detailed information on all sorts of things that do not concern us at this stage; see Appendix 4 for details. For the moment all we need know is that power boats must keep out of the way of ('give way to' is the usual expression) sailing boats, unless they are large enough to be restricted in their manoeuvring by a narrow channel or whatever. Most commercial shipping in harbours and narrow waterways come under this category and you should keep well clear of them. Even

at sea it can be difficult for large ships to get out of the way of small sailing boats, so it is prudent to always give them a wide berth. Alter course in plenty of time so that the ship can clearly see that you are steering to avoid him, or he might suddenly alter course at the last minute and create dangerous confusion. Sailing boats must also give way to boats fishing, and boats carrying out complex operations such as dredging, minesweeping and flying off aircraft. Details of the signals shown by vessels engaged in such activities will be found in a Nautical Almanac (see Appendix 3).

If two sailing boats are on course for a collision the one on port tack must give way to the one on starboard tack. If they are both on the same tack the one to windward must give way. If a sailing boat is motoring (even with her sails set) she is classed as a boat under power for the purpose of these regulations and must act accordingly. She should also hoist a special signal to indicate this (see Appendix 4). If one boat (of any type) is overtaking another, it must keep clear. In general, all vessels should keep to the starboard sides of channels.

5

Tides and Anchoring

There will be many times, for various reasons, when you will be unable to tie up to a jetty or a mooring buoy. At such times you will have to go out into the harbour and tie yourself to the seabed somehow. We do this with a heavy metal object known as an **anchor**, which is designed to hook itself firmly into the bottom, and we tie ourselves to it with a long rope or chain, known as an **anchor warp**. Anchoring properly, so as to ensure that we do not drag away in strong winds or tides, or swing around banging into jetties or other boats, requires some skill and knowledge. The anchor must be the right type and weight; the warp must be the right size and length; the water must be the right depth; and the chosen spot must be sheltered from wind, waves and strong tides. See photos 26, 27 and 28 for information on anchors and warps.

Figure 37 shows a boat anchored the way it should be. The anchor is firmly dug into the seabed and the chain cable is neatly laid out in a line along the bottom. There are three good reasons why the warp should be laid out neatly like this. First it ensures a horizontal pull on the anchor which will tend to dig it in all the time rather than pulling it up and out. Secondly, the friction of the chain lying on the bottom reduces much of the load

on the anchor. Thirdly, the long length of chain on the bottom can lift to absorb shocks if the boat lurches violently in waves or strong winds, thus reducing the chance of a sudden violent snatch jerking the anchor loose or straining a fitting on board. Nylon warps absorb this snubbing by their ability to stretch considerably.

The boat will lie like this, pointing usually into the tide as she would on a mooring, while the wind will cause her to lie sideways, or sail up and over the anchor so that the warp leads aft. With the anchor laid properly none of this should affect her security. As the tide turns from ebb to flood, or vice versa, so the boat will swing round with it much as she would on a mooring, although in a much wider circle.

Tides

As the tide floods into harbours so it rises in height, then falls again as it ebbs out. Clearly this will affect not only the amount of anchor warp we should **veer** (let out) but also the places where we can anchor (or we might go aground at low water). Let us look at tides again, in a little more detail this time.

We mentioned in Chapter 4 that the tides were caused by the gravitational pull

Photos 26–28 Three different types of anchor commonly used in small boats. The **Danforth** anchor in Photo 26 and the **CQR** anchor in Photo 27 are generally used as main anchors due to their very effective holding ability in most conditions. The traditional **Fisherman** anchor in Photo 28 is commonly used in dinghies and as a **kedge** (spare) anchor in large boats as it folds up for stowage. It holds better in rocky or weedstrewn bottoms than the other two. As a general guide the weight of an anchor in pounds should be a bit more than the length of the boat in feet: a 30ft boat should carry a 35lb anchor. The kedge is normally a bit lighter so as to be more easily manhandled when carried away in the dinghy to haul off when aground etc (see Chapter 11). Suitable sizes of warp and chain will be recommended by suppliers, so ask your local chandler or boat-yard. Although much research is done into the holding powers of various anchor types, there is little doubt that the more weight you have on the bottom the better. So carry anchors as heavy as you can manage, with chain on the main one and nylon on the kedge (for ease of handling).

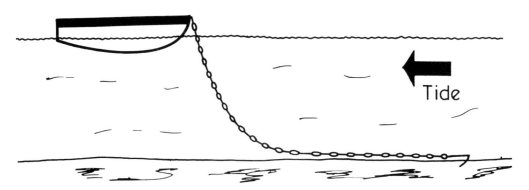

Tide

Figure 37 This boat is anchored with chain cable, which should be at least three times as long as the depth of water. With nylon warp this **scope** (as it is called) should be at least five times the depth. Nylon is more easily lifted off the bottom than chain so more scope is needed to maintain the necessary horizontal pull on the anchor. It should have a chain 'leader' of at least five metres between it and the anchor – partly to ensure the horizontal pull on the anchor, and partly to prevent the nylon chafing on the bottom. Because of the lighter and longer scope, a boat anchored on nylon will roam around a lot more than will one on chain, so more swinging room must be given. Anchor chain should be marked every five metres with paint, and nylon with small line tied securely through the lay.

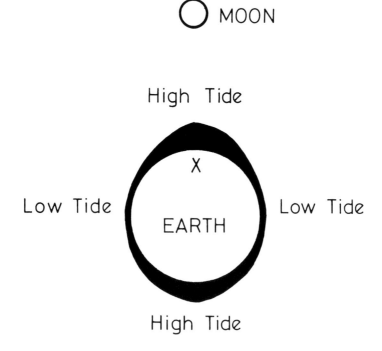

Figure 38

of sun and moon. The moon, being much nearer to the earth than the sun, has the greater effect, and we can see this effect in figure 38. At points on the earth's surface in line with the moon the water is pulled up, so raising the sea level to High Tide. Elsewhere the level is lowered to Low Tide as the water is drawn away to where it is being raised. As the earth revolves completely once every twenty-four hours, it should be apparent that the point marked X will go through a sequence of High Tide, Low Tide, High Tide, Low Tide and back to High Tide again, with the water level steadily falling or rising during the six hours between each extreme. See figure 39.

If the earth rotated in exactly twenty-four hours and the moon stayed still, that would be the end of that. However, the solar system is not quite that simple. The earth does not revolve in exactly twenty-four hours; the moon does not stand still, but rotates around the earth every twenty-eight days (roughly); the whole shooting match goes round the sun about once a year; and doubtless the sun goes round

something else now and again. All of which conspire to prevent the tides occurring at the same time every day, with a neat six hours between High and Low!

In figure 40 we see more or less what happens (as it affects us in practice). During the moon's 28 day revolution around the earth the apparent movement of the sun is very small. Thus the gravitational pulls of the sun and moon are in line twice and at right angles twice. When they are in line (top and bottom of figure 40) the combined pull on the tides is strongest and we find High Tides to be very high and Low Tides very low (because more water is being pulled away to the very High Tide elsewhere). When sun and moon are at right angles the combined pull is least, giving relatively low High Waters and relatively high Low Waters, there being less overall movement of water. The tides with the big **range** (difference between High and Low Water heights) are called **spring tides**, and those with the small range are **neap tides**. In between there is a gradual change from one to the other. Tidal streams will be

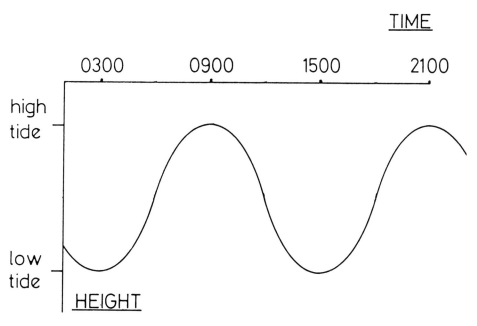

Figure 39

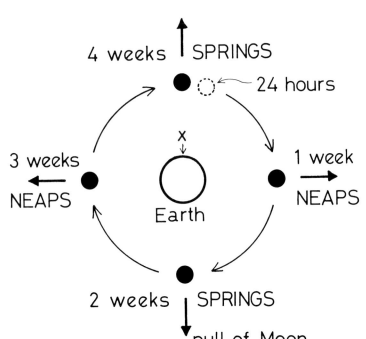

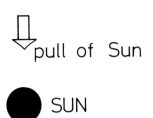

Figure 40

strongest during spring tides (due to the greater volume of water being moved between High and Low Waters), and weakest at neaps.

Furthermore, if we look at the dotted moon at the top of figure 40 it should be apparent that after 24 hours the point X on the earth, having made one complete revolution, will no longer be directly under the moon. It will, in fact, have to turn a bit further to get under the moon and produce the next High Tide – another 50 minutes roughly. (In one day the moon will move 1/28th of its 28 day rotation, and to catch up with it the earth must move 1/28th of its 24 hour rotation; ie about 50 minutes.) Thus High Water is about 50 minutes later each day.

These are the most important variations in the tide that concern us, but there are many more minor ones preventing the tides adhering rigidly to even this changing pattern. For example, when sun and moon are in opposition, spring tides are not quite so high as when they are in line; and twice a year we get very big spring tides, known as **equinoctial springs**. They occur around the time of the **spring and**

autumn equinoxes (21st March and 23rd September) and are often accompanied by bad weather – the so-called **equinoctial gales** whose existence is vehemently denied by the meteorologists but sworn to by very many experienced seamen!

To sum up, we can say that we have a High Tide twice a day with a Low Tide roughly six hours after each one; and each day these tides are about fifty minutes later than the previous day. Every month, a couple of days after the full moon (when it shows as a complete white circle) we have Spring Tides, when High Tide is very high and Low Tide very low, and tidal streams very strong. The range of the tide (difference between High and Low Tide heights) and the speed of the tidal streams steadily decrease over the next week to a minimum at Neap Tides, when High Tide is relatively low and Low Tide relatively high. The range and the strength of the streams then steadily increase again over the following week until a couple of days after new moon (just a very thin line round the moon is visible) when they once again reach a maximum at the next spring tides. They then fall again towards a minimum at the next neap tide (at neap tides the moon shows as a crescent). And so on every month. You will find that spring tides occur at much the same time of day in a particular place, as do neaps.

Information on times and heights of the tides for various places can be found in **Tide Tables**, published annually both locally and in various **Nautical Almanacs** (see Appendix 3). Not only do the times of the tide vary between different places, but the range can also change dramatically, due to geographical influences. The spring range at Gibraltar is little more than a foot, while that in the Channel Islands can be as much as forty feet.

Calculating Depth of Water

When we pick a spot in which to anchor we must be sure that the boat will float at Low Water and that we will have the required amount of warp out at High Water. For these purposes we need to know the depth of the actual water, which is not the same as the height of the tide. The height of tide, as given in the tide tables, is measured above a certain level known as **Chart Datum**, which is an arbitrary position generally just below the level of the lowest spring Low Water. Maps of the sea, known as **charts**, have depths of water marked on them and these are measured below chart datum (more on charts in Chapter 10). Thus the actual depth of water that we experience when on a boat is the sum of the charted depth and the tidal height at the time. Charted depths are generally referred to as **soundings** unless they rise above chart datum, as they do in the shallows, when they are called **drying heights**. Depth of water over a drying height is thus the tidal height *minus* the drying height. Soundings are usually marked in metres and tenths of metres on modern charts, and drying heights are underlined. See figure 41.

In figure 42 we have a chart of Runswick Bay in North Yorkshire. There is a lot of information on this chart that will assist us in selecting a suitable spot to anchor. The land is at the bottom and to the left, and you can see that the area of chart showing the sea is covered in numbers, lines and letters. The numbers show depths below chart datum (unless underlined, when they are above chart datum). The lines, much like contour lines on a land map, join places of equal depth, and are known as **depth contours**. You should be able to pick out the 1 metre line (dotted), the 5 metre line, the 10 metre line and so on. Inside the 1 metre line you can see a ragged, rocky-looking line running around the bay. In places it is interspersed with short lengths of contour line, and on one such length at the top left of the bay you will see the figure 0. This is, in effect, the zero metre line: ie chart datum, and most depths inshore of this are underlined, being drying heights above chart datum.

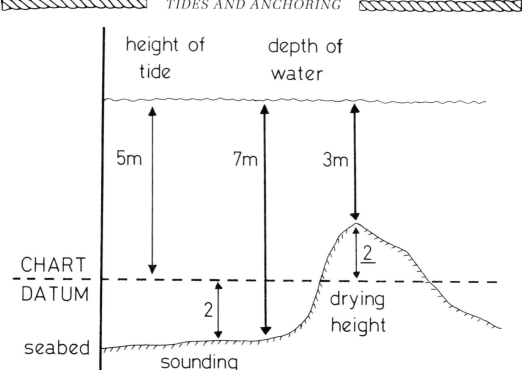

Figure 41

Before we can safely anchor the boat, we must know not only the actual depth of water at that time and place, but also how much higher it might rise, and how much lower it might fall while we are there. The actual depth can be found either 'on site' by measuring it when we get there (we will see how shortly), or by picking a suitable spot on the chart and calculating what the depth there will be when we get to it.

To find the actual depth of water where we are we can use either a **leadline** or an **echo-sounder**. The former is simply a long rope with a weight on the end, marked at intervals to show the depth. We lower it over the side till the weight hits the bottom and read off the depth from the mark at the surface. See figure 43. An echo-sounder is an electronic gadget that sends a pulse of sound downwards from the bottom of the boat. This rebounds from the seabed and is picked up by the **transducer** (the fitting under the boat that

sends out the sound), and passed through a wire back to the echo-sounder. Knowing the speed of sound in water, the echo-sounder then calculates the depth from the time the pulse took to go to the bottom and back. They can usually be adjusted to display the depth below the transducer, the depth below the keel, or the depth below the surface, whichever you find most convenient to work with. I would suggest depth below the surface as this makes tidal calculations a lot easier. Echo-sounders are much faster and more efficient to use than leadlines, but do have limitations – they cannot tell the depth anywhere other than directly below the transducer, and they can break down. So you should always carry a leadline as a standby. Unless two transducers are fitted – one each side of the boat – echo-sounders can be rather inaccurate when the boat is heeled over a lot, as the pulse then shoots off at an angle to strike the seabed some way from the boat.

To find out how much this depth will alter while we are at anchor, we must

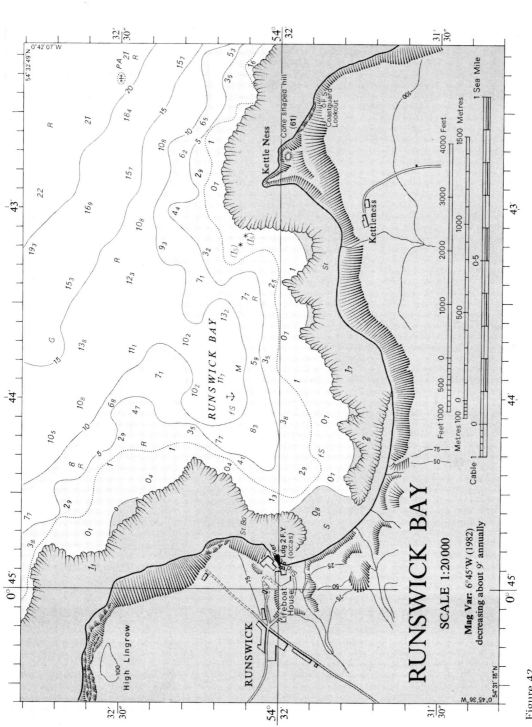

RUNSWICK BAY

SCALE 1:20000

Mag Var: 6°45'W (1982)
decreasing about 9' annually

Figure 42

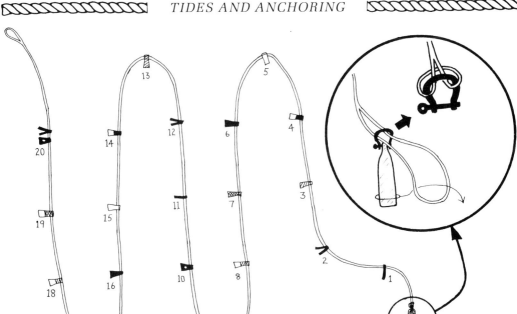

Figure 43

know how the tidal height will vary, as the sounding will not change. If we anchor at exactly High or Low Water, the tide tables will give us the height. At any other time we must work it out. Fortunately the tidal height changes fairly predictably in most places, and steadily between High and Low Water, so this is not difficult. In figure 44 you can see that the tide rises slowly to begin with, increases speed considerably over the period around half-tide, then slows down again as it reaches High Water. The same happens when it falls. If we divide the range by twelve, you can see that in the first hour of the flood the tide will rise by one twelfth of its range; in the second hour by two twelfths; and in the third hour by three twelfths – making six twelfths (a half of its range) by half tide. It then steadies and slows down its rate of flooding, rising three twelfths again in the fourth hour; two twelfths in the fifth hour; and the final twelfth in the final hour. This is known as the Twelfths Rule and it

is most important that you remember it. It is not scientifically accurate for a number of reasons, but it is perfectly adequate for our purposes, as a good safety margin of depth should always be allowed to take into account waves, atmospheric conditions affecting the height of tide and so on. More accurate methods of calculating tidal heights can be found in Nautical Almanacs, and are essential in certain places that have abnormal tides. See the Almanac for information on these.

The Anchorage

Let us imagine we want to anchor in Runswick Bay (see figure 42). There are two basic criteria for a good anchorage – the comfort of the crew and the safety of the boat. Both of these are fulfilled by shelter from wind, waves and tidal streams, and a seabed which provides a firm grip for the anchor. Clearly, if the wind was blowing straight from the sea into this bay **(onshore wind)** at any strength it would be far too rough for an anchorage, especially as the waves would

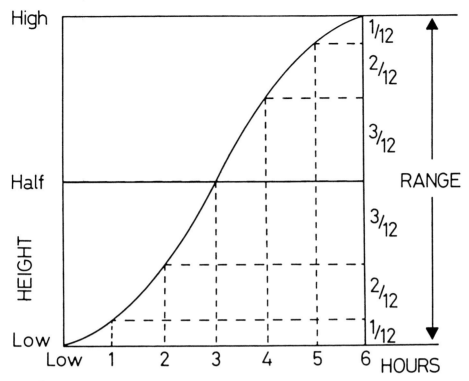

High

Half

HEIGHT

Low

Low   1   2   3   4   5   6 HOURS

1/12   2/12   3/12   RANGE   3/12   2/12   1/12

Figure 44

get much rougher on rolling into the shallow water (see Chapter 9). With wind off the land **(offshore wind)**, however, the high ground around the bay (see contour lines) would provide excellent shelter, and there would, of course, be no waves. If the wind is from an intermediate direction things are not so clearcut. We may be able to tuck tightly into a corner of the bay, out of the direct line of wind and waves, but in practice waves often bend round into a bay and, although no longer directly wind-driven, the rolling **swell** can be both uncomfortable and unsafe. A swell (waves not pushed by the wind – often the dying remnants after a wind has dropped) can also be in evidence even with an offshore wind, making an apparently sheltered anchorage quite untenable. Only experience can teach all this, so do not be too quick to commit yourself to an anchorage until you have gone in and looked at it.

There will be little or no tidal stream in a bay like this, as the main stream along the coast will shoot straight past the mouth of it. Information on tidal streams can be found on charts and in booklets called **Tidal Stream Atlases** (see Chapter 10). The nature of the bottom can be deduced from the small letters dotted about amongst the soundings. The ragged-looking grey area around the bay is rock, and you can see the letters St. Bo just off Runswick village, meaning stones and boulders. To the bottom right of the village is a smoother area with S marked on it for sand – this is clearly a beach. Further out in the bay we find fS for fine sand, M for mud, R for rock, G for gravel, and so on. Details of all chart symbols and signs can be found in a **Nautical Almanac**, a book containing vast amounts of information on tides, harbours, signals and so on (see Appendix 3). By and large, good holding ground for an anchor can be found in sand, thick mud and clay, while rock, weed and fine sand or soft mud are

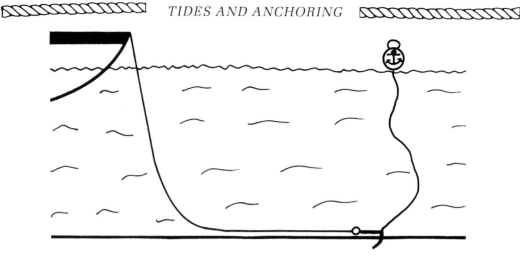

Figure 45

not so good. Some anchors are better than others at holding in poor ground (see captions to photos 26, 27 and 28). In the middle of the bay, just below the name, you can see a small anchor marked on the chart. This indicates that the holding ground here is especially good – it appears from the symbols to be a mixture of mud and fine sand.

We must also beware of anchoring where the bottom is **foul** – where old wrecks might be lying – or where telephone or power cables are laid, as the anchor might get trapped. Both these dangers will be marked on the chart. Other causes of trapped anchors are rocky bottoms and mooring chains from large buoys or anchor cables from other boats. Give all these a wide berth, and if in doubt about the bottom use a **buoy rope** on the anchor. This is a light line attached to the **crown** (bottom end) of the anchor and kept afloat by a small buoy or fender. See figure 45. If the anchor fouls, this line can be hauled on to pull it backwards out of the obstruction. Make sure the line is long enough to reach the surface at High Water or the rising tide could pull on it and loosen the grip of the anchor. Paint an anchor on the buoy to prevent others from mooring up to it. It happens!

Having decided that Runswick Bay (or a sheltered part of it) will make a suitable anchorage, we must calculate (using the Twelfths Rule) the actual height of the tide for the time of our arrival, so that we can work out how much higher it will rise to High Water and how much lower it will fall to Low Water. The former will tell us the scope of anchor warp to use, and the latter will tell us how close we can go in without grounding at Low Water. If we calculate that on arrival the tide will have two metres to fall to Low Water, then we must anchor with at least this depth under our keel, plus a safety margin of, say, another metre. So we must look to anchor in a depth of three metres minimum plus our **draft** (depth to bottom of keel from surface).

With a draft of one metre we must then let go the anchor in four metres of water. If the tide then has another two metres to rise to High Water, we will at that time find ourselves anchored in six metres of water, and this is the depth for which we must calculate length of anchor warp. Bear in mind that if we intend lying at anchor for more than one tide, the heights of both High and Low Waters may change during this period, so all calculations must be made for the highest High Water and lowest Low Water likely to be experienced during the stay at anchor. In this instance a minimum of 18 metres of chain or 30 metres of nylon must be veered with

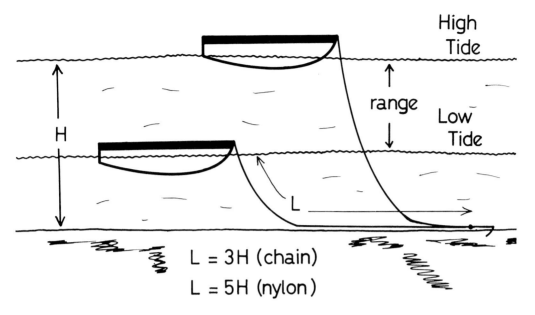

Figure 46

the anchor. See figure 46. Remember that at Low Water all this surplus warp may allow us to swing a long way from the anchor, so leave plenty of room clear of rocks, other boats and shallow water. It is no good anchoring in the required depth if at Low Water you swing into water too shallow to float. Try to judge from wind and stream which way you will be lying as the tide ebbs, and ensure that you do not lie over a shallow patch.

These same tidal calculations will have to be made if we berth alongside a quay in a tidal harbour, to ensure that we do not ground at Low Water. Do not listen to the 'local' who tells you there is 'plenty of water here'; sometimes there is and sometimes there is not! Work it out for yourself.

Letting go the Anchor

The actual mechanics of anchoring are not difficult, and the approach to the chosen spot should be made as though it were a mooring – ie into the tidal stream or wind, whichever one you judge you will lie to when anchored. See Chapter 4. With wind and tide together, some practice and experience will be needed to gauge the precise moment to round up head to wind so that you will coast to a stop at the chosen spot. You should then let go the anchor and hand all the sails so that they do not fill with wind as you fall back away from the anchor. You will find that the bow will blow off sideways as you drift astern, so this is most important. Veer just enough warp to get the anchor firmly on the bottom, then veer the remainder steadily as she falls back, to ensure that it lies out along the bottom and does not pile up in a heap on top of the anchor. If you have a proper **windlass** (anchor winch) you can probably do this with the brake; otherwise control the veering of the cable by firmly resting a foot on it as it lies on the deck, varying the pressure to let it run or slow down. NEVER do this with bare feet or loose flip-flops – rough edges on chain will rip you to shreds and nylon will burn your flesh as effectively as a blow torch! With the required amount out you can secure it to whatever cleat or **bollard** you have on the foredeck – the largest and strongest. In Chapter 6 you will find details on securing anchor warps, preparing the anchor, and so on. Then hang a **bow fender** round the bow to protect it from chafing by the warp as you swing and move about. With wind and tide in opposition or at an angle, approach the anchorage under jib only, just as for approaching a mooring buoy.

If the anchor has not set properly then there is the possibility that in strong winds or tides it will drag along the bottom under the strain. Good basic anchoring technique will do much to reduce this danger, but it must always be watched for. When the boat has settled to her anchor you should have a good look round to see where you are lying in relation to other fixed objects such as mooring buoys, houses or trees ashore, and suchlike. A regular check on this while at anchor should then show if you are dragging out of position, although allowance must be made for the boat swinging round in changing winds and tide and generally ranging about on the end of the cable.

Weighing Anchor

This is the nautical expression for hauling it up again. Before setting any sails you should first haul in cable until about twice the current depth is left out. This is known as **shortening in** and it simply reduces the amount of time you spend with the sails flapping about. You then set the sails you would for leaving a mooring, depending on the directions and strengths of wind and tide, weigh the rest of the cable and sail off. If, however, you are head to wind and space dictates that you sail off in one particular direction, you will find this more difficult than doing so

from a mooring buoy, due to the problem of assessing precisely when the anchor lifts off the bottom thus allowing you to sail away. A constant check must be kept on the amount of cable out in relation to the depth. When it is nearly equal to the depth, you must patiently wait until the boat swings off in the right direction before making a final rapid heave to clear the anchor off the bottom while she still points the right way. The jib can be judiciously backed at the crucial moment to ensure that the bow swings as desired.

If the anchor sticks in the bottom so that you cannot haul it up, there are various techniques for clearing it. One is to get all the crew for'ard to trim the bow down, then haul the cable taut and secure it, then send everyone aft. With luck the buoyancy of the bow springing up again will pull it clear. If the tide is rising and you are in no hurry, then simply secure the warp and wait for the rising tide to either pull the boat under the water, or pull the anchor out of the bottom (preferably the latter!). The other alternative is to sail or motor the anchor out by brute force, manoeuvring so as to yank on the anchor from such an angle that the warp pulls on it in the direction opposite that in which it is dug in. To do this under sail you will need to veer the warp again to its original length, then sail off to one side until it comes taut; tack (or turn) and sail hard back towards the anchor. When you come up taut on the warp the next time, the force should hopefully heave it loose, whereupon you can hand sails if necessary and weigh the anchor normally. If you do try to shift the anchor with brute force (using sail or power), then leave the bow fender in position to protect the hull from the chain.

6

Knots and Seamanship

The tying of knots properly is a vital part of sailing: hardly a moment goes by without one being needed for some reason or another. When used on boats it is important to appreciate that considerable and complex strains can often come on knots, so the correct one must always be used for a particular purpose. There are various factors that must be considered before choosing a knot for a particular job: it must not slip or fall apart under strain; it must not slip or fall apart when flapping violently in the wind; it must not slip or jam when wet; and it must be easily undone when required. Let us look at the common uses for knots on board the boat and see what knots will do those jobs best.

Knots and Lashings

Tying the boat up to a buoy or a jetty is perhaps the first task to spring to mind, and the best knot will depend on the type of fastening point available. Securing to a buoy involves tying up to a metal ring and the main requirement here is that the knot grips the ring firmly; if it is loose it can slide back and forth on the metal and wear away the rope. The knot you should use here is called a **Round Turn and Two Half Hitches** and you can see the way it is tied in figure 47. Apart from holding securely

in all conditions, this knot has two qualities that make it particularly suitable for tying into a ring: if tied tightly it will not move and chafe against the ring; and it can easily be undone while still under strain.

When tying up to a jetty or marina pontoon you may also find metal rings for mooring to, in which case this knot should again be used. If large cleats or bollards are available, however, a better knot is the **Bowline**, which makes a loop in the end of the rope which can simply be dropped over the cleat or bollard. This loop can slide about, but with the relatively large surface area of a bollard this will not induce chafe, and the simple loop is easier to handle than a round turn and two half hitches. This knot cannot be untied while under strain and can jam after long periods under tension, so should never be tied *into* anything, only dropped over things. If a relatively small cleat is used the eye should be doubled before putting it over, so as to reduce the movement and chafe. See figure 48. To double the loop simply twist the eye at the bottom so it forms an 8, then lay the bottom circle over the top one. Work the double eye round the cleat so that all parts are under even strain. If the cleat is open in the middle, you can pass the eye

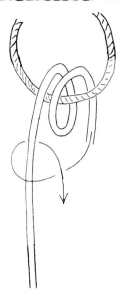

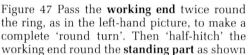

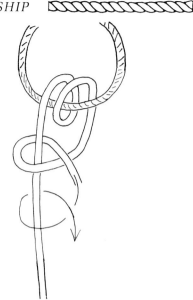

Figure 47 Pass the **working end** twice round the ring, as in the left-hand picture, to make a complete 'round turn'. Then 'half-hitch' the working end round the **standing part** as shown

by the thin arrow, and draw the knot up tight. Finish with a second half-hitch as shown by the thin arrow in the right-hand picture.

Figure 48 Form a small eye in the standing part about twice as far from the working end as the diameter of bowline required. The standing part should emerge from the back of this eye, so that the finished knot holds it tightly against the eye: see left-hand drawing. Then feed the working end round as shown by the thin arrow, and tighten the knot (right-hand pic-

ture) by hauling up on the standing part and down on the working end and the right-hand part of the loop together. Any loose bits should then be worked through until all parts fit snugly together, and a few inches of working end protrude (to ensure it cannot shake apart). There is a quick way to tie this knot, but it is difficult to describe; get someone to show you.

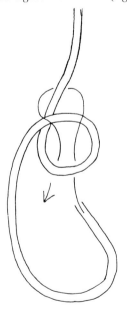

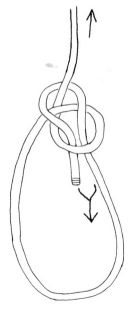

through the middle then loop it back over the outside to get a similar effect. If another bowline is already on the bollard you must **dip the eye** of the second up through it before putting it over. This will enable the first eye to be removed without having to lift off the second. See photo 29.

The **Reef Knot** is a well-known knot, much in use ashore for joining two ropes together. At sea, however, it should *never* be used for this purpose as it can capsize under strain and fall apart. It is used for tying **reef points** in a sail as explained in Chapter 9, and for no other purpose except wrapping up birthday presents. See figure 49. A **Sheet Bend** is the knot for joining two ropes and it can be seen in figure 50. The **Clove Hitch** is a useful knot when used in its proper role of a 'crossing knot', but it is often vaunted as just the thing for tying lanyards to buckets, and fenders to guardrails, when the round turn and two half hitches is very little more trouble and infinitely more secure. Probably the most useful purpose of a

Photo 29 The second eye to be placed on the bollard is tucked up through the first one before being slipped over the bollard. This should be done at all times, whether securing to a jetty or to a boat, as it enables the first eye to be removed without disturbing the second (which may be under strain). If more than one eye is on the bollard, then you must dip yours through all of them: that way any one can be removed without disturbing the others.

clove hitch is for lashing the tiller, when a lanyard can be secured on one side of the cockpit, clove-hitched to the tiller, then the end hauled taut and secured on the other side of the cockpit. It should *never* be used for mooring a boat, however small. See figure 51.

When a boat is rolling and leaping about in waves it is most important that all gear should be securely lashed to prevent it flying around. Spare coils of rope should be tied up as in figure 52 and large objects on deck, such as dinghies, can be lashed down very tightly using **Waggoner's Hitches**. See figure 53.

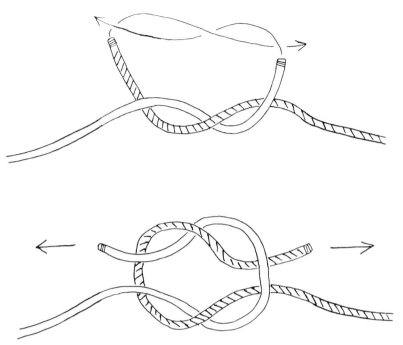

Figure 49 Take the ends of the lines one in each hand and lay the left across the right; then tuck the left down round the back of the right and up the front, as in the top picture. Take this same end and cross it over the other (now on the left), then down and through as before, shown by the thin arrows. Draw the finished knot (in bottom picture) tight by hauling on all the parts as shown, keeping the knot symmetrical.

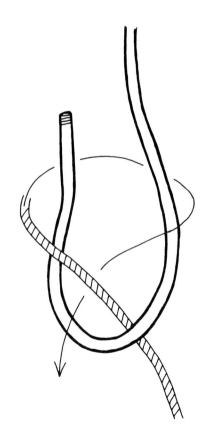

Figure 50 Put an open loop in the end of the thicker of the ropes to be joined. Pass the other rope up through and round the back of this loop, so that both short working ends come out on the same side of the knot – as shown by the thin arrow. If they come out on opposite sides it is a **Weaver's Knot**, which is less secure. Then tuck the end under itself as shown and draw up tight. A **Double Sheet Bend** has the end passed round the same way a second time, and is a more secure knot (see photo 30). When the loop is an eye, as here, it does not matter from which side the working end protrudes.

Photo 30

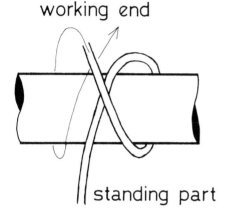

working end

standing part

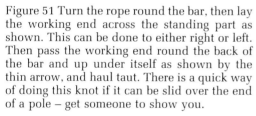

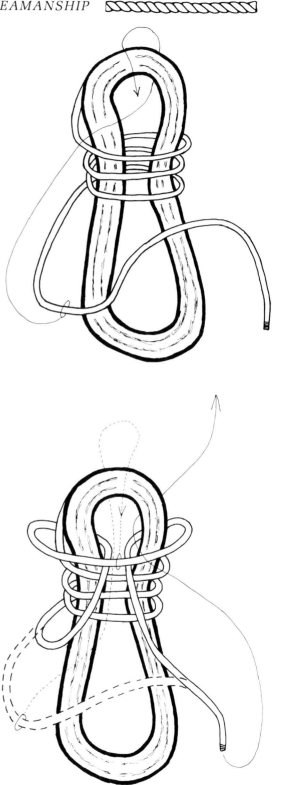

Figure 51 Turn the rope round the bar, then lay the working end across the standing part as shown. This can be done to either right or left. Then pass the working end round the back of the bar and up under itself as shown by the thin arrow, and haul taut. There is a quick way of doing this knot if it can be slid over the end of a pole – get someone to show you.

Figure 52 Hold the coil in your left hand with the loose end hanging down the back. Turn the loose end round the bight of the coil a few times as shown in the left-hand picture, and haul taut. Then pass the bight (middle bit) of the working end through the coil above these turns, leaving the end dangling down the front, and pull the bight forward over the top of the coil. Follow the thin line in the left-hand picture and the thin dotted line in the right-hand one. Haul everything tight, then pass the working end itself through the coil above all the turns, as shown by the thin arrow in the right-hand picture, and pull tight. The coil can be carried, or hung up, by this working end.

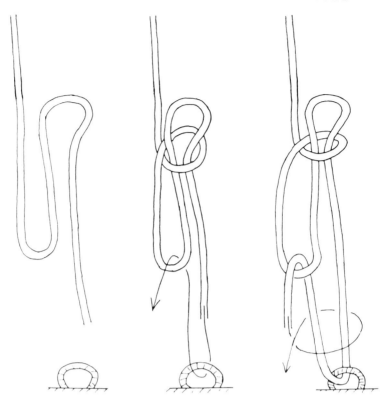

Figure 53 Take a bight of the rope close to the attachment point and haul it up alongside the standing part as shown in the left-hand picture. Then make a small eye in the standing part just below the top of this bight (as you would for a bowline) and tuck the bight up through it as in the middle picture. Then pass the working end through the attachment point and up and through the bottom of the loop formed, as shown by the thin arrow in the middle picture. Haul down as tightly as possible on the working end, then secure it with a couple of half hitches as shown by the thin arrow in the right-hand picture.

Another useful way of tightening a lashing is by frapping (hauling it sideways) as we saw on the halyards in Chapter 3. Finally, let us look at a much underrated knot which enables you to haul sideways along a rope, spar or whatever – the **Rolling Hitch**. See figure 54. There are countless uses for this knot, but perhaps the most important is for taking the strain on a jib sheet that has jammed with riding turns on the winch. A line can be rolling hitched onto the sheet, passed round the jammed winch and across the cockpit, to be hauled tight on the other winch. With the weight of the sheet removed from the riding turns they can be cleared fairly easily, replaced cleanly on the winch and the weight taken again before releasing the rolling hitch.

Mooring to a Buoy

There are two types of mooring buoy you are likely to encounter, the most common being a large plastic buoy with a hefty metal ring at the top. To tie to one of these you should pass a rope (secured to a cleat on the boat at one end) through the ring and back to another cleat on the boat. This is called a **sliprope** and is solely to hold the boat temporarily while you secure her properly with a hefty warp and a round turn and two half hitches (see above) or, better still, a length of chain shackled to the ring (both very strong and resistant to chafe). See figure 55. To stop the boat rubbing against chain or buoy, slip a length of plastic hose over the chain or haul the buoy up close to the stemhead. The sliprope should then be left slack. When you slip from the buoy, tighten up the sliprope and disconnect the main warp from the ring. The sliprope can then be quickly and easily let go when required. Slipropes are also useful when leaving an alongside berth as they enable the final warps to be released from onboard. If they are led through ringbolts on top of the wall, the end leading from the top of the ring should be let go and the one underneath hauled on to slip. If you pull on the top end it will jam the ring down onto the other end and the rope will not move. If the ringbolt is in the side of the wall, you should haul on the end nearest the wall for the same reason.

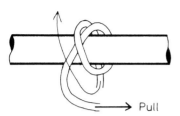

→ Pull

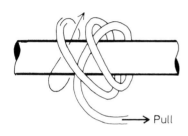

→ Pull

Figure 54 Take a turn round the spar or rope as you would for a clove hitch. The working end, however, *must* come up the front on the side of the standing part nearest the pull, then be crossed away from it as shown. A second turn is then taken as shown by the thin arrow, and this must be pulled tightly into the space between the first turn and the standing part — or the knot will not grip. The knot is finished similarly to the final turn of a clove hitch, as you can see by the thin arrow in the bottom picture, the turn being made and tucked on the opposite side of the standing part to the first two turns.

Figure 55 A **shackle** is a U-shaped piece of metal with a hole in the end of each arm, one of them threaded. It is closed by screwing a pin through the two holes. You will find it in use all over the boat for joining things together. The thread should be kept lightly greased to stop it seizing up, and shackles fitted permanently — rigging, anchor cables etc — should be moused with stiff wire as shown, to prevent the pin unscrewing. If the shackle is underwater it should be **moused** with wire of similar material to prevent corrosion — see the section on **electrolysis** in Chapter 12.

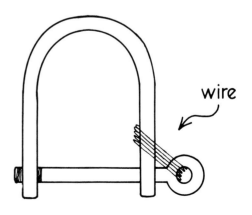

wire

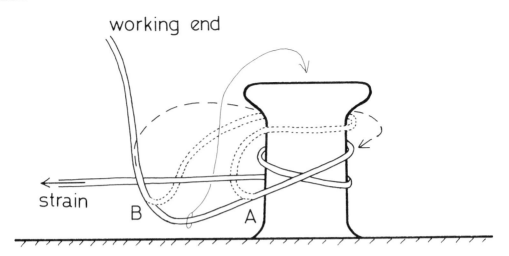

working end

strain

B   A

Figure 56 A **Tugboat Hitch** is an excellent way of securing chain or heavy rope to a single bollard, as it is quick and easy to do and can never jam. If you have taken a couple of turns to hold the boat, this knot can then be made without having to slacken off the turns. With two or three turns on the bollard, take the strain at A with one hand then tuck a bight of the working end under the standing part and over the bollard as shown by the thin arrow and the dotted rope. Shift this hand to B ready to take the strain, then let go at A. The technique is similar to dropping an extra turn on a winch. You should now have sufficient friction to take the strain mostly on the bollard and further similar turns can be added for security after passing the working end round the back of the bollard as shown by the thin pecked line so that it leads as it did originally. The knot is undone by simply unravelling the bights from the bollard, keeping the strain on the working end, until the original few turns are left, when the rope can be safely **surged** under any remaining strain. It is ideal for towing as it can be so easily and quickly let go in emergency.

The other type of mooring you may find (less often these days) is a small plastic job without a big metal ring. This will be attached to a length of rope leading to a chain on the bottom, which is the actual mooring. Haul up the buoy and the rope till you reach the chain, then secure the chain round your mooring cleat or bollard. See figure 56. If in any doubt as to which type of mooring buoy it is, haul it up and look underneath to see whether rope or chain is attached to it. If the maximum size of boat the mooring will hold is not painted on the buoy then compare the size of the chain with your anchor chain. To be safe it should be at least as big. It is not a bad policy while checking the chain to inspect the big shackle attaching it to the bottom of the buoy. This is very prone to corrosion, being alternately in and out of the water, and you should ensure that the pin is not worn away where it bears against the chain. If in any doubt, go and find another mooring.

Mooring Alongside

When we lie alongside a jetty or pontoon the boat must be tied up in a certain way in order to hold her securely. Four ropes are generally used, as you can see in figure 57, and each has a particular purpose –

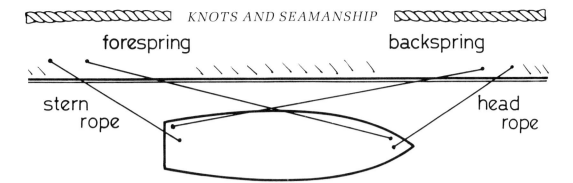

forespring   backspring

stern rope   head rope

Figure 57

they do not simply 'stop the boat drifting away'. In principle we can say that the **headrope** stops the bow moving away from the jetty, the **sternrope** stops the stern from doing the same, the **forespring** stops the boat moving forward, and the **backspring** stops her from moving back (although some authorities reverse the names of the springs). As a general rule the springs should be hauled in as tightly as possible to hold the boat still and stop her rubbing back and forth along the berth, and the head and stern ropes given a little slack to allow for the boat pitching in the wake of a passing vessel. The springs should be as long as possible, so that their length will absorb any movement of the boat, while head and stern ropes should lead to the quay at roughly 45°. If necessary they should be taken from the outside of bow and stern to get this angle right; too great an angle will not permit sufficient movement in passing waves, while too small an angle will not hold bow and stern in properly. If there is noticeable range of tide, then warps must be left long enough to allow the boat to rise and fall with it. Long springs then come into their own as they can be kept tight and still absorb considerable vertical movement of the boat, while holding her alongside. When lying outside another boat, head and stern ropes should be led to the shore as well as to the other boat, so that his lines do not take the full weight of both boats. This also enables him to slip out without casting you adrift.

Fenders should be distributed evenly along the hull to spread the load if the boat presses hard against the berth. Try to have them against an internal strongpoint such as a bulkhead, and make sure they are at the right height. Hang them from the bases of stanchions, not from the guard-rails, which could be put under unfair strain. Put fenders near bow and stern to allow for either end swinging into the jetty, which is what happens if springs are not rigged correctly. A backspring should be led tightly from the stern of the boat so that the weight of wind or stream pushing the boat backwards comes on the spring, which both holds her in position and keeps the stern in. The headrope will stop the stern swinging in too far. If the spring is not rigged like this, the strain will come on the headrope, which will pull the bow tightly into the wall. The same applies to the forespring.

In rough weather double up all the warps to reduce the strain on each, ensuring that the pairs are evenly tensioned so that they share the load. Protect all mooring warps from chafe wherever they pass over anything the slightest bit rough or sharp – edge of the quay or deck, corner of a fairlead and so on. You would not believe how much a warp can chafe on a wild night even in the smoothest of fairleads. Wrap them with thick cloth or old rope, or slit lengths of plastic hose and clip them over the rope at appropriate places, including the eyes of bowlines and eye splices where they bear against the bollard. This also applies to mooring buoy pendants and nylon anchor warps.

Handling Ropes and Lines

It is important to realise that many of the ropes and lines that you handle onboard the boat are likely to be under considerable tension, and if handled incorrectly can cause damage to both the boat and the crew, as well as making a mess of the current manoeuvre. There are two basic aspects to this: the possibility of a rope under strain running away with itself; and the virtual certainty that given half a chance any rope that is slack will wrap itself firmly around every obstruction it

Photo 31 Take the weight with one hand (the left here) fairly close to the winch and pass a loose turn round the barrel with the other. Then let go of the bight and heave taut rapidly on the working end. The turn should slide neatly round the barrel without your fingers getting close enough for danger. Practise it in quiet conditions so that when it is needed in earnest you have the confidence to do it quickly and safely.

can find. When handling a rope that can come under strain – mooring warps and sheets mainly – always be ready to take a rapid extra turn round the winch, cleat or bollard if you feel extra strain coming on – *before* the strain gets too much for you to hold. These turns must be wound on carefully so that control is always maintained and the strain kept on. If a rope once starts to run away with you it will be extremely difficult to control, not to mention dangerous. If a rope needs making fast quickly – a stern rope to stop the boat for example – then do not waste time trying to tie a knot but just get a few turns rapidly round a handy bollard or cleat and lean back hard against it to take the weight.

Putting an extra turn on a winch or bollard under load can be fraught with risk, as it is difficult to keep strain on the working end while at the same time turning it round the barrel. If there is enough space, you can simply wind it round while leaning back hard to hold the

weight – keeping your fingers well clear of the turns in case the rope slips a little. If you have no room to safely do this without leaning over and risking losing balance, then a turn can be put on as shown in photo 31. It is equally important to control and keep the strain on a rope while easing it out, and this can be difficult to do smoothly if there are too many turns on a winch or round a bollard. Turns can be assisted to render round a winch by pushing them round with the palm of the hand, keeping the fingers well clear, but there is no safe and simple way to remove a turn – it must be carefully unwound while keeping control of the strain. You may see very experienced seamen quickly flick the top turn off then heave back to hold the strain, but do not try it until you are equally experienced!

It is worth practising the art of throwing lines as the ability to get one ashore or to another boat quickly and cleanly could save getting into trouble. This is best done by splitting the coil in two and taking one half in each hand. The half in the throwing hand wants to be as small as possible so that it will fly well through the air. Throw this half and let the rest run out freely from the other hand. If your mooring warps are rigged as shown in figure 58

before you approach a berth, you will then be able to secure them instantly and properly the moment the shore end is made fast, and they will be able to safely take strain immediately as they will be in position in their fairleads. Always have the inboard end secured to a cleat to prevent losing it when the other end is hauled on. The same arrangement should be used for anchor warps, so that the anchor can be simply lifted and thrown over the rail. The inboard end of the cable should be secured inside the chain locker with a long rope lashing that will reach up on deck if the cable is run right out. It can then be cut if you have to clear the anchorage in an emergency (large ship about to crash into you perhaps).

Any warps or cables that are to be run out any distance from the boat (anchor warp; kedge warp being rowed out by dinghy etc) should be **flaked** down rather than coiled, as this enables them to run out more easily without tangling. The anchor chain should be hauled out of its locker and ranged in parallel rows on the deck, as long as possible, so that no part lies on top of any other. It will then run freely without tangling. When weighing anchor, you should endeavour to flake the cable as it goes into the locker, each layer

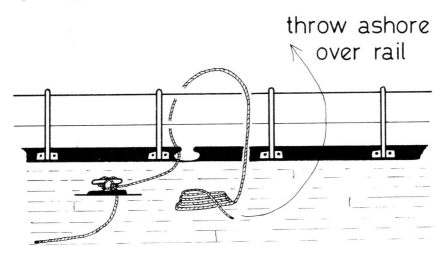

throw ashore over rail

Figure 58

Photo 32 A rigid fibreglass dinghy, being rowed easily and comfortably by a youngster. Practice makes perfect: get someone to show you the proper technique. This young lad should really be wearing a buoyancy aid (see Chapter 7).

Photo 33 A proper inflatable, designed specifically as a yacht tender. Note the built-in rowlocks, and the two black fittings on the stern to take the bracket for an outboard motor. Between these, on the inside of the dinghy, is an inflation valve. There should be at least two separately inflated chambers, to provide reserve buoyancy in case of puncture. The rope hanging along the side of the dinghy serves both for carrying and for a man in the water to hold onto.

Photo 34 A well loaded inflatable dinghy motoring with a small outboard. On a wild and windy night this would be too many people unless the water was very calm and sheltered all the way out to the boat.

of chain being ranged at right angles to the previous one. Then if you have to anchor in a hurry, and have no time to flake the cable on deck, it should hopefully run out without jamming. Rope is best flaked in large loose figures of eight, each one slightly smaller than the one below it so the rope runs out from the middle to begin with, and steadily works outwards as the pile is depleted.

The Yacht's Tender

When anchored or moored out in a harbour some means of getting ashore is needed, not only for shopping and suchlike, but also for emergencies. We need to carry or tow a small **dinghy**, which we can row with oars or drive with an **outboard motor** (more on engines in Chapter 12). There are two basic types suitable for small cruisers – rigid dinghies built of generally fibreglass or wood, and inflatable dinghies built of special rubber

tubes that can be blown up with a simple pump. The former are tough, and they row and motor well; while the latter are prone to damage on rough beaches etc, row abominably, motor slightly more efficiently, but have the great merits that they are very light to carry and can be deflated and stowed in a small space. See photos 32 and 33. An inflatable should be a proper 'yacht's tender' and not a 'child's beach toy' which will not be strong or stable enough, nor feasible to row in anything other than a flat calm. For a small yacht this can also double up as a **liferaft** on coastal passages, being more suitable for this purpose than a rigid dinghy as it is less likely to capsize or sink. See Chapter 7.

It is an illuminating fact that more yachtsmen are drowned from dinghies in harbour than are ever lost at sea. A dinghy is a small unstable device that needs to be handled with great care, especially in exposed estuaries and at night. Never indulge in horseplay in a dinghy, or even stand up if it is avoidable. When getting in or out, hold it securely at both bow and stern and step straight into the middle, then sit down. Get all passengers settled in and sat down, and the dinghy trimmed

and balanced properly before leaving shore or boat. Do not overload it or it will feel sluggish and unstable, and will not ride waves safely; the risk of capsize or swamping will be greatly increased. See photo 34. At night or in rough weather wear – or at least carry on board – **buoyancy aids** (see Chapter 7). Carry also a powerful torch and shine it about at night so others can see you. Carry spare oars and **crutches** (rowlocks), baler, anchor and warp (all tied to the boat in case of capsize), as well as long **painters** (mooring ropes) permanently secured at bow and stern. An inflatable should also carry a pump and an emergency repair kit in case of punctures.

When tying up a dinghy ashore remember to allow for range of the tide, and make sure, if securing at Low Water, that the painter is fastened above the High Water position! Use a round turn and two half hitches. An inflatable dinghy can generally be left to rattle around on the end of its painter, being in effect a floating fender, but rigid dinghies can get bashed about quite badly in rough weather when secured to an exposed jetty. They can be held clear of the jetty by throwing the anchor out astern as far as possible and

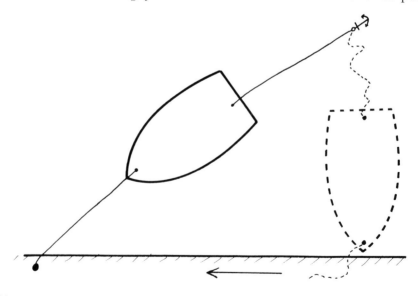

Figure 59

securing the warp to the stern. Then walk along the jetty with the bow painter and secure it far enough along that the dinghy is held clear of the jetty by its anchor. To get back aboard, simply walk back along with the painter until you are opposite the anchor, when the shorter distance will permit the bow to reach the jetty. See figure 59. This also keeps the dinghy away from landing steps that others may want to use. A second, very long bow painter is useful for this, and for high walls with large tidal ranges. Strong permanent fendering on a rigid dinghy is a sound idea.

Outboard motors on dinghies should be secured with a strong safety line in case of capsize or dropping overboard. Always fasten this line before lowering the motor over the stern, in case you drop it! When not in use the outboard should be tilted clear of the water to avoid collecting weed, to prevent damage if the dinghy grounds, and to reduce resistance when rowing. Shut off the fuel and the fuel breather in the cap or the stuff will pour out into the dinghy; petrol is highly inflammable, dangerous stuff. In confined spaces tow the dinghy on a very short painter, or you may find it going a different side of a buoy or moored boat to you; which can be very embarrassing. Carry the dinghy on board at sea if you possibly can; they are a menace to tow in waves as they roam about all over the place in imminent danger of capsize. If you have to tow, then do so with two painters, one to each quarter of the cruiser, and adjust their lengths so that the dinghy is on the crest of a wave at the same time as you. This will reduce sheering, strain on the painters, and the risk of capsize or swamping.

7

Life Aboard the Boat

Two important factors make living aboard different from life ashore, and we must be constantly aware of their significance if sailing is to be both safe and enjoyable. The first is that a boat floats in the water, and for our well-being and comfort we must ensure that she continues to do so. Water belongs outside a boat, and if it gets inside in sufficient quantities the boat will sink. Thus it is most important that we have at least one system for pumping out water. Pumps for this purpose are known as **bilge pumps**, because they pump water out of the **bilge** (the bottom of the boat). Although some types are more reliable than others (being less likely to jam on sucking in foreign objects), all can be improved dramatically by fitting a strainer on the end of the suction pipe that lies in the bilge. This should be easily accessible for regular cleaning. Try to keep the bilge clear of rubbish anyway; few pumps can pass bits of old rag, wood shavings or even water if the **strum box** (strainer) gets clogged with such things.

All boats should have at least one powerful hand-operated bilge pump – preferably the diaphragm type which is very simple, reliable and repairable – situated in the cockpit where it can be used by the helmsman; the rest of the crew might be furiously baling out with buckets and saucepans in a real emergency! A second, similar pump provides extra pumping power and is also a very seamanlike standby in case the first fails. A further pump, belt-driven off an in-board engine, has the twin merits of shifting large amounts of water rapidly, and not needing a man to pump. With these three you will be well equipped.

The other factor that makes life on a boat so different from life ashore is that if something dreadful happens – like a fire – you cannot simply run out of the front door and down the street screaming for help. So not only must you be extra careful to avoid the risk of fires when out on the water, you must also be equipped and able to tackle them yourself if they do occur. Basic firefighting techniques are discussed in Chapter 11, but here let us consider the equipment we should carry on board, and the precautions we should take to reduce the risk of fire.

There are three main areas of fire risk on board a boat; fuel (especially petrol); gas if your cooker runs on bottled gas, as most do these days; and cooking fires (fat in frying or chip pans). The first two carry the added risk of explosion.

The major risk with the first two is that both petrol fumes and gas are heavier than air so slight leaks will run down and gradually accumulate in the bilge. Sooner or later this will mix with the air down there to form an explosive mixture which can be set off by the slightest naked light, such as a pilot light, cigarette or even a spark from a dropped spanner or an electrical switch being turned on or off. This danger can be reduced almost to nil by the simple expedient of pumping the bilges daily until the pump starts sucking air; then continuing with a further dozen strokes or so, thus pumping out any residual gas or fumes. For this reason it is also good policy to pump the bilges like this immediately you go aboard after an absence – before lighting cookers, cigarettes and so on.

Other precautions are equally simple. All gas bottles (including spares) should be kept on deck from where any slight leaks can drain overboard. When changing a bottle smear a little soapy water over the connection – bubbles will indicate the smallest leak. Always shut gas off at the bottle when not in use. Petrol for outboards should also be stowed on deck in approved cans and kept as far as possible from the cockpit (where people might smoke). Large amounts for an inboard engine should be kept only in properly designed integral tanks. When fuelling (even with relatively safe diesel) there should be a total ban on all naked lights (cigarettes, cookers, pilot lights and so on) however far they may be from the fuelling point; and no machinery of any kind should be running, because of the risk of sparks. For the same reason no electrical switches should be turned on or off during refuelling. The delivery nozzle should rest against the metal of the filler pipe to provide an earth for static electricity, and the pipe itself must be earthed to the tank, which in turn should be earthed to the engine, which must be earthed to the water (see section on electrolysis in Chapter 13). Swill a bucket of water over the deck round the filler before beginning operations, then any spillage will float on this film of water and thus wash away easily. On completion of fuelling, pump bilges dry as described above, to remove any fuel or vapours.

By adhering to these simple precautions, and ensuring that the galley stove is shielded from draughts that might blow the flame out, we will reduce the risk of fire to almost negligible proportions. If we then equip the boat properly with firefighting equipment we will have done everything humanly possible to protect the boat and her crew from such dangers.

In view of the likely risks outlined above, all extinguishers should be capable of dealing with fuel fires. Dry powder, foam or inert gas are the most common and their relative merits will be discussed in Chapter 11. At least two should be carried and some careful thought given to the siting of them. The best extinguisher in the world is of no use at all if the fire prevents you from getting to it! Consider where fires are likely to start – engine room, galley, deepest part of the bilge (explosion from accumulated fumes) – and site extinguishers so that wherever you are in the boat at the time, you can reach at least one without being cut off or beaten back by the fire. The same thinking should be applied to the siting of a fire blanket, an essential item somewhere near the cooker, which can be rapidly draped over a fire in a pan to exclude the air. *Do not* put it tidily behind the cooker, thus requiring you to lean over the fire to get to it; or hide it neatly where no-one can see it. Have all extinguishers checked at the recommended intervals by the supplier (they do not remain efficient for ever), and *read the instructions when you buy them*; do not wait until the boat explodes in the middle of a black night with a gale blowing! The only fire I have experienced on a boat was accompanied by an explosion that burnt all the instructions off the extinguishers.

Medical problems can also be considerably magnified by being a long way from a doctor. In serious cases help or advice may be summoned by radio-telephone as explained in Appendix 4. Very often a doctor can tell you what to do over the radio, or he can be brought out by lifeboat or helicopter, or ferried from a nearby ship. Most of the time, however, a competent skipper should be able to cope with first aid procedures on his own, and I strongly recommend that you attend a first aid course to gain experience in resuscitation techniques and so on. A well-equipped first aid box should be carried on board, painted white with a large red cross and stowed somewhere handy, and visible. A list of contents will be found in a Nautical Almanac or a yachtsman's first aid book (see Appendix 3), and one or other of these reference manuals should also be carried. Ready made first aid kits sold for use in cars are not adequate for taking to sea.

Accommodation

With those potential horrors under control we can now relax and enjoy the cosy comfort that only a boat can offer. In figure 60 we see the layout of a fairly typical modern cruiser about 28 feet long that can sleep four in comfort, and six at a pinch. This size of boat will almost certainly have the cockpit at the stern, with all the accommodation for'ard of it; although larger ones may have a second small cabin right aft. The latter type will be steered with a wheel and the former most likely by tiller. Wherever the cockpit is situated it will have seating around the sides, under which there will be storage lockers. In these should be stowed items such as fenders, mooring warps, leadline, spare emergency tiller, deck scrubbers, fishing lines, buckets and so on – anything likely to be used on deck. Some boats keep sails here and some keep them right for'ard, from where they can be readily hauled out of the for'ard hatch. At least one bucket should have a line secured to it so that it can be lobbed over the side to collect water for scrubbing decks, peeling potatoes and so on. This needs to be done with some care if the boat is moving or you could be dragged over the side by the pull of the water on the bucket. Throw it

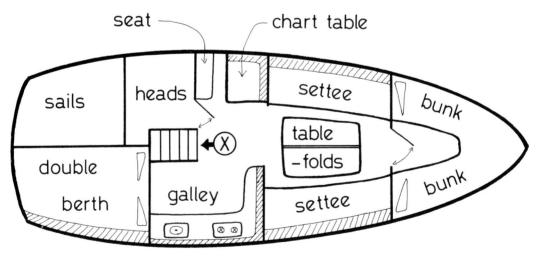

X = steps to cockpit
– engine under

Figure 60

forward so that the bucket lands in the water upside down, then heave it clear of the water before it draws astern and begins to drag.

A **boarding ladder** should also be stowed somewhere handy, and it should be long enough to reach at least a couple of feet below the surface when hung over the side. This will enable a man in the water to get his feet on the bottom rung to assist him in the strenuous heave clear of the water. Make sure the ladder fits securely over the edge of the deck and have a short line fitted each side so that it can be lashed firmly into position. Care is needed when swimming from a boat. Never do so in a strong tidal stream as it could easily sweep you away. With any tidal stream always swim upstream of the boat so that if you get tired you will be carried towards the boat rather than away from her. When children are swimming have the dinghy in the water manned by a capable rower, in case they get into difficulties. *Never* use an outboard engine, or have the yacht's auxiliary running (even in neutral) because of the serious risk of a swimmer getting caught in the revolving propeller. Gearboxes often 'creep' in neutral, thus turning the prop slowly, and it is all too easy for someone to knock the gear lever. Young children can gain confidence in the water, and have a lot of fun, by swimming in their buoyancy aids (see later in this chapter), and this is a good way of testing their efficiency. It is most important that a child's buoyancy aid cannot slide up over the shoulders when in use in the water. Make sure that the buoyancy aids are thoroughly dried out afterwards as some types can become waterlogged after long immersion.

From the cockpit we go through a hatchway, that will likely have removable boards slotting into the entrance and a sliding hatch over the top, and into the cabin – a process known as **going below**. The interior layout of small cruisers varies considerably, but there will be a number of bunks (some doubling as seats in the saloon), a **galley** (kitchen), a chart table (for navigating – see Chapter 10), a tiny bathroom with **heads** (WC) and wash-basin (possibly even a shower), and a variety of stowage areas. The engine is usually under the cockpit floor, with access from inside the cabin. Under the saloon floor will likely be a fresh water tank with a filler pipe leading to the deck. Pumps in the galley and heads will draw water when required, although some boats may have pressurised systems allowing for the use of normal taps. The heads work rather differently from a WC ashore, pumping water from outside the boat to fill the bowl, then pumping the whole lot out of the boat again, having mashed it all up in the pump. Some boats may pump the residue into a **holding tank** which is then pumped out ashore at special stations in boatyards. This is normal on inland waterways where it is not permitted to discharge effluent into the water.

It should be apparent that space will be very much at a premium, and it is most important to be tidy and well organised, keeping gear stowed away securely so that it does not fly about when the boat is rolling and pitching at sea. It is also important to realise that a number of holes exists in the bottom of the boat (sink drains, heads inlet and discharge etc) which could sink you if water is allowed in through them. Special valves known as **seacocks** can close off these holes when not in use, and they should be closed at all such times, in case a pipe falls off or corrodes. Boats can get damp inside when not used often, and ventilation is important; ideally there should be a vent right forward and one right aft, so that air flows all through the full length of the boat. Sleeping bags and clothes should be stowed in plastic bags and galley equipment susceptible to moisture (matches, salt etc) are best kept in airtight containers.

Boats roll and pitch when at sea – quite violently at times in rough weather – and there should be strong handgrips all over

Photo 35 A typical buoyancy aid, with a zip front and extra securing ties. Some types have buoyancy round the back of the neck as well (to keep the head afloat). Children should have this type, and also ties beneath the legs to stop it sliding up over their heads.

Photo 36 This is a simple and effective life-jacket for use in small boats, that restricts the wearer's movements very little. For inflation it is opened out at the front and blown up by mouth, although some types have small gas bottles built in that inflate them. Note the buoyancy round the back of the neck.

the saloon to enable you to move about safely. There should be a harness arrangement at the galley so the cook can strap himself in and wedge himself against the movement, and there should be **fiddle rails** to keep pots on the stove, and to prevent things sliding off tables and work surfaces, and secure catches on all doors and lockers. Damp cloths are very effective anti-slip devices as well. There should be some system to prevent the crew from falling out of their bunks – either canvas **leecloths** that can be lashed up at the outside of the bunk, or permanent wooden **leeboards** about ten inches higher than the mattress. Ideally, bunks should be no more than about two

feet wide, thus enabling a sleeper to wedge himself firmly; double berths may be cosy in harbour, but they are no use at sea, unless they can be split by a central leeboard.

Safety Equipment

Besides engine, anchors, warps, heads and so on, there are certain other important items of equipment that should be carried on board. Buoyancy aids – buoyant waistcoats that help to keep a conscious person afloat in the water – should be carried to fit all members of the crew. They should be worn, properly secured, by children at all times, and by adults in

circumstances such as rough weather, night, fog, and by inexperienced swimmers. See photo 35. **Lifejackets** are rather more complex (and expensive) devices designed to keep an unconscious person afloat with head clear of the water. They are not essential for estuary cruising and short coastal hops, but should be carried in preference to buoyancy aids for sailing offshore. See photo 36. **Harnesses** should be worn at all times in rough weather and at night (even when sat in the cockpit), and by children while they play. Safety lines should be adjusted so that when

Photo 37

Photo 38 A selection of distress flares, all with detailed instructions printed on the sides – *read them before going to sea.* From left to right we have a red parachute flare, a red hand flare, and an orange smoke float (thrown in the water it produces dense orange smoke for daylight use). White hand flares are similar to red but with white caps instead of red ones.

clipped onto a strongpoint (not a guard-rail) the wearer is prevented from going over the side. See photo 37.

Flares are rather like large fireworks that can be set off to attract attention when you are in trouble. Three types should be carried on board, in a strong watertight container stowed somewhere handy in the cockpit. White flares should be used to attract the attention of a passing vessel for advice or assistance, or to warn him of your presence, while red flares should be used only in a real emergency involving the risk of losing the boat or crew. There are two types – parachute flares and hand flares. The former fires a red flare to a great height and it then drifts slowly down on a parachute. They should be used when no vessel is in sight as they can be seen from a considerable distance. Hand flares have a very limited range of visibility as they simply produce a flare from the end of the stick held in the hand. They should be used on approach of a vessel, enabling him to pinpoint your position. All flares should be fired downwind; this keeps heat and debris from hand flares clear of your face, and enables parachute flares to reach a greater height. Read the instructions carefully before you have to use them! Always replace by the expiry date shown, as out-of-date flares can be dangerous or useless. They should be handed to the police or local coastguard – do not put them in the bin or throw them overboard. See photo 38.

Radar reflectors are curious devices that increase dramatically the size of echo your boat will produce on a ship's **radar** screen (see Appendix 2). Small boats can easily not show at all on radar, especially in bad weather when many echoes from waves can mask those from small boats. Reflectors should be hoisted as high as possible in poor visibility or at night, although I would strongly suggest that they are permanently mounted high up on the mast; even in good daytime weather a small boat can be difficult to see from the bridge of a large ship. There are two basic types available – the cheap and reasonably effective traditional type and the expensive and very effective modern type (see photos 39 and 40). It is most important that the traditional type be hung up in the right attitude (so that signals can enter the indentations squarely and be reflected back to their source). Place the assembled reflector on a flat surface so that it rests on the three corners of an indentation, and this is how it should hang on the boat.

For offshore cruising you should carry a proper **liferaft** in case you have to abandon ship in rough weather. For estuary and coastal cruising the dinghy should suffice – an inflatable being better for this purpose than a rigid dinghy. When you are at sea, have it stowed or towed so that it can be got into and paddled away as rapidly as possible in case you have a fire and possible explosion to get away from. Take the flares with you so that you can attract attention.

Wherever you cruise there is always the danger of someone falling overboard, so two **lifebelts** should be carried in holders, one on each side of the cockpit where they can be quickly reached by the helmsman. At least one should have a light attached to it in case a man has to be recovered at night. It is quite impossible to find someone in the water at night without a light to guide you. Special floating lifebelt lights are obtainable that switch on automatically on being thrown into the water. See photo 41.

A **foghorn** should also be carried and it needs to be as powerful as possible, if it is to be heard on the bridge of a big ship from a safe distance. If you have good electrics and charging system I recommend an electrical one with a mouth-operated standby. Small aerosol types are better than nothing, but not much.

Personal Equipment

When you are sailing, remember that you cannot pop back into the house for anything you have forgotten, so make certain

Photo 39

Photo 40

Photo 41

you have everything you might possibly need. Besides checking that you have sufficient water, gas, food, engine fuel and so on, you should also carry plenty of warm, water- and wind-proof clothing for all the crew, towels and at least one complete change of clothing each. Even on a nice sunny day it can be surprisingly cold on the water, and there is always the likelihood of getting wet. Equally, the power of the sun is much stronger at sea than on land, due to increased ultra-violet rays, and the cooling effect of wind will disguise the true burning strength of the sun. Limit sunbathing to begin with and use a good suntan barrier cream or lotion. Glare can also make steering and looking out difficult, so sunglasses can be useful. See Appendix 1 for detailed lists of the equipment you should carry.

8

Weather Forecasting

There are two main types of weather forecast available which predict the likely conditions out at sea. There is a specialised **Shipping Forecast**, specifically tailored to the needs of sailors, and there is the general land forecast, usually more concerned with the likelihood of rain than anything else. Our concerns, by and large, are the wind direction and strength, and the visibility (risk of fog). The shipping forecast should be our staple diet, with land forecasts (as we shall see) as useful additions.

The Shipping Forecast

This is broadcast regularly on BBC radio and details of times, programmes and frequencies are given in Appendix 4. It is always read out in the same format, consisting of:

Gale Warnings: a list of sea areas in which gale force winds are expected.

General Synopsis: a brief description of the weather chart (such as they show on television), from which the forecast is calculated. It gives the experienced listener a general picture of the overall weather pattern which enables him to deduce the implications.

Area Forecasts: these give specific information on wind strength and direction, the general weather and the visibility expected during the next twenty-four hours in the areas of sea marked and named in figure 61. The forecasts begin with Viking and work clockwise round to South-East Iceland.

Station Reports: these give present weather conditions at a number of observation posts around the coast. The information comprises wind direction and strength, general weather (if of interest; eg heavy rain), visibility, and atmospheric pressure together with indication of how it is changing. The positions of these coastal stations are shown in figure 61, although not all the stations are always used.

Interpreting the Forecast

There is a considerable amount of information in this forecast, large tracts of which are totally ignored by far too many small boat sailors. All too often a skipper will check from the chart which area he is sailing in, then merely listen to the forecast for that area, ignoring everything else. And that is one reason why so many of them get into trouble. Let us look in some

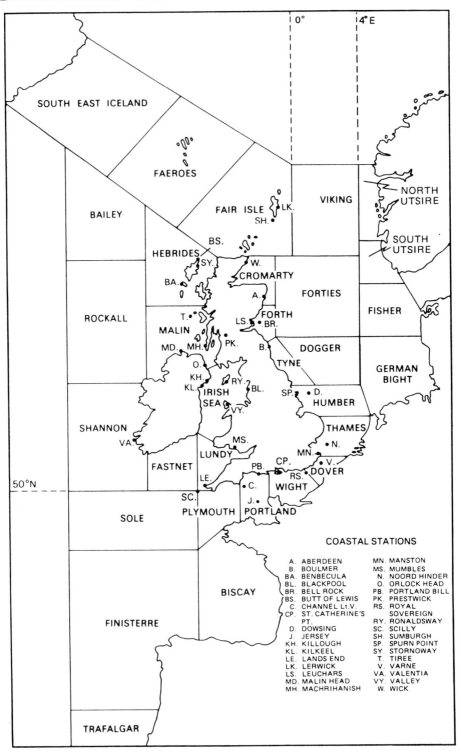

Figure 61

detail at this shipping forecast and see just how much we can learn from it.

There are two most important points to appreciate. One is that meteorology is not an exact science. A meteorologist will be the first to tell you that he cannot predict precisely what the weather will do next. All he can do is assess, using his training, experience and information, what he thinks the weather is most likely to do. The two are not the same. The other important point is that by the time the forecast is read out over the radio it is already some hours old. If it is broadcast at 1750, it will have been issued by the Met. Office about 1700, and their predictions will have been calculated from synoptic charts drawn up at midday and at three in the afternoon. Important information, however, can be inserted into the forecast as late as 1700. I trust, though, that the point is made: the shipping forecast is not infallible.

In principle, the weather is caused by the interaction of regions of different atmospheric pressure. Air, generally, will flow from high pressure regions towards low pressure regions, just as water flows from high places down towards low ones. The intermingling of these airstreams – some dry, some wet, some warm, some cold – generates energy and produces the weather; and that is as deep as we are going to delve into the theories of meteorology.

The General Synopsis tells us about these different pressure regions – where they are, speed and direction of their movements, how low or high the pressures are at their centres, and how steeply the pressures rise or fall away from the centres. In general, low pressure areas – known as **lows** or **depressions** – bring wind and rain, while high pressure areas – **highs** or **anticyclones** – bring light breezes and fine weather. These regions can usually be seen quite clearly on a weather map, surrounded by roughly circular lines (see figure 62). The lines, called **isobars**, are drawn to join places

with equal atmospheric pressure (much as map contour lines join places of equal height); the actual pressures (in units called **millibars**) are written on the lines which can be seen wandering all over the place on a television weather chart. Although the air flows generally from high pressure areas to low pressure areas, it ends up swirling round the centres of these areas, anticlockwise round a low and clockwise round a high in the Northern Hemisphere. In the Southern Hemisphere these directions are reversed. Thus the wind that we actually experience on the water (which is simply this movement of air) blows more or less along the isobars; although in practice the rotation of the earth throws them a bit off course and they end up blowing slightly inwards towards the centre of a low and outwards from the centre of a high. See the arrows in figure 62.

The speed of the wind is governed by the steepness of the pressure change. If the isobars are close together, the pressure is falling steeply towards the centre of a low or the outside of a high. The wind will blow hard down this gradient, just as water flows rapidly down a steep hillside. When the isobars are far apart, as they usually are in a high, the wind will blow slowly across this gentle gradient. In the area forecasts the speed of the wind (more commonly known as its strength) is given not in miles per hour but in a simple code known as the **Beaufort Scale** (see Appendix 4). This scale also gives descriptions of the likely state of the open sea in each wind strength. Although Force 8 is described as a gale it must be borne in mind that Force 6 is a lot of wind for a small sailing cruiser, and is often referred to as a 'yachtsman's gale'. Even Force 4 in certain conditions can be a frightening handful for an inexperienced sailor on the open sea. See Chapters 9 and 10.

Wind direction is given in terms of north, south, east and west, together with various directions in between. These are shown in figure 63, and a study of this

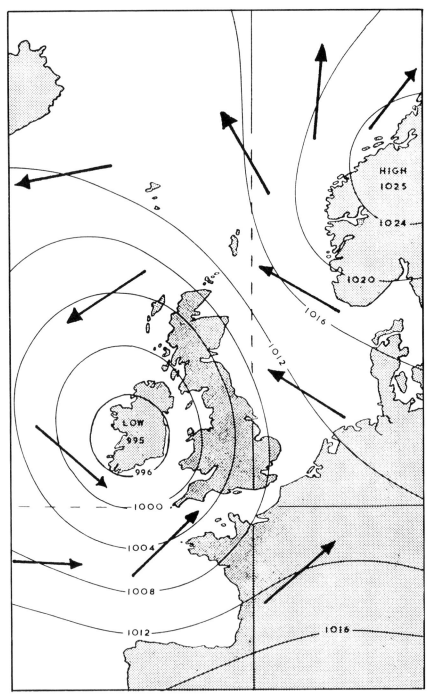

Figure 62

compass rose, as it is called, will show the logic of the intermediate directions. North-east is midway between north and east; north-north-east is midway between north and north-east; north by east is just a little to the east of north, and so on. The wind is always described as coming *from* a particular direction: the north wind blows *from* the North Pole, not towards it. That is why it is cold!

Atmospheric pressure is measured on a device known as a **barometer**, and is often referred to as the barometric pressure. There are various types of barometer, but the commonest in use on small boats looks somewhat like a clock and is known as an **aneroid barometer**. It is absolutely essential to have one of these on board as it can give you all sorts of information about the impending weather. If, for example, the pressure on the barometer (often called **the glass** as early mercury barometers looked like large glass thermometers) suddenly begins to fall rapidly, you can be certain that this denotes the approach of a deep depres-

sion, with its attendant strong winds, perhaps gales, and rain (see Appendix 4 for more detailed information). The glass will fall until the centre of the depression is over you, then rise again as it moves away. This will generally denote a better spell of weather, if only for a day or so; although it is important to appreciate that a rapidly rising glass can produce just as strong winds as can a rapidly falling one. A study of the **synoptic chart** (weather map) will tell you what is to follow the passage of the depression.

Depressions

Most of the time, depressions approach the British Isles from the west, travelling at speeds of anything up to thirty knots or more. Usually, the deeper the depression the faster it travels, so the worst weather tends to pass over quite quickly (gales lasting hours rather than days). As the depression approaches, the barometer falls and the cloud begins to gradually thicken, building up from the west. If the

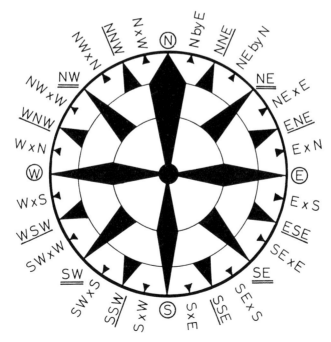

Figure 63

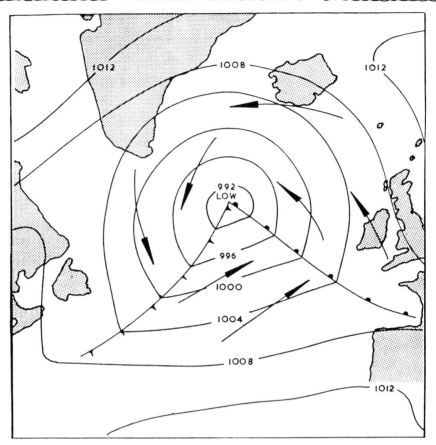

Figure 64 The **Warm Front** is on the right, marked by half-round blobs. It is so called because it brings warm air behind it – in the triangle between the fronts known as the **Warm Sector**. The **Cold Front** is on the left, marked by points, and is so called because it brings cold air behind it. It is the interaction of the warm and cold air masses that causes these fronts. The arrows across the isobars show the wind directions around the depression.

depression is heading to pass north of us (and most of them do go north of Britain), the wind will **back** (shift anti-clockwise) and begin to freshen up from the south, or possibly the south-east if the depression is further south than usual. It will then gradually **veer** (swing round clockwise) into the south-west, getting stronger all the time. This is the time when the wind is usually strongest, as the depression is

nearest to us then (see the wind direction arrows in figure 62). As the depression moves away to the east or north-east so the wind will gradually decrease, at the same time continuing to veer towards the west and sometimes as far as north-west. The barometer begins to rise as the higher pressure isobars move towards us, and the cloud will move away with the depression, leaving clear blue skies, dotted perhaps with white fluffy 'cotton wool' clouds.

Often these depressions will contain **fronts** (see figure 64). The fronts mark dividing lines between different types of airstream, and they have the effect of altering the gradual change described above to two quite distinct and sudden changes. Before the warm front the wind will be moderate south or south-east, the cloud will be reasonably high still and just beginning to thicken and there will likely be no rain as yet. As the warm front passes over, you can see from the way the isobars kink that the wind will shift suddenly into the south-west, then the clouds will thicken considerably and it will begin to pour with rain, often sufficient to reduce visibility quite drastically. At the same time the wind will blow up much harder and the barometer will slow down its rapid fall. This happens because the isobars in the warm sector are more or less parallel to the track of the depression, so as it passes over the pressure remains steady.

As the cold front passes over, the cloud often ceases so abruptly that you can see a clear line of blue sky approaching from the west as it gets near. As this line goes over, the wind will immediately fly round into the west or north-west and the barometer will begin to rise, sometimes quite rapidly. With a strong cold front a south-west gale can be followed by a north-west gale for a time, although it usually quietens down fairly quickly. Remember, the steeper the pressure gradient the stronger the wind, whether the glass is rising or falling. So watch your barometer at all times and keep track of its movement by noting the pressure in the ship's **logbook** hourly (see Chapter 10). In Appendix 4 you will find a guide to what the barometer's rate of change can tell you.

If the depression passes to the south of us we will not have these dramatic frontal changes, and the wind will shift differently. If you look carefully at figure 64 you will see that the wind will start off easterly and will then gradually and steadily back through north-east to about north. The barometer will fall till the wind is about north-east, then begin to rise. It will rain heavily, continuously and drearily the whole time, and visibility will almost certainly be poor due to this rain. If the actual centre of the depression is going to pass directly over your sea area

then **cyclonic** winds will be forecast. This simply means that the wind will shift rapidly and steadily from about south-east to north-west, veering or backing depending on whether the centre is slightly south or north of you. Look at figure 64.

Anticyclones

An anticyclone is quite different from the action-packed depression. Usually much larger, it drifts about rather aimlessly, often appearing to form, disintegrate and reform again whenever the mood takes it. With widely spaced isobars it generally produces light winds or calms, and as it does not contain the vigorous, swirling and interacting airstreams that constitute a low, little cloud is formed within it. The summer characteristics of a high are thus light breezes, clear blue sky and sunshine. In short, just what the skipper ordered.

Due to their lack of energy and determination, highs tend to be pushed around and swallowed up by every passing low of any intensity. Occasionally, however, we find a strong high that stands its ground, forcing all the lows approaching from the west to divert north or south around it. This is called a **blocking high** and is the cause of the long fine settled periods we sometimes find in summer around the British Isles.

In these conditions we often experience what is known as a **sea breeze** – wind blowing in from the sea with no regard for isobars, that is caused by the sun heating up the land and the air close to it. This hot air then rises and cooler air is sucked in from the sea to take its place. This sea breeze generally begins late in the morning (when the sun has had time to heat up the land) and continues until early evening, when the sun cools down and the rising of warm air from the land ceases. During the day the sea breeze gradually veers (clockwise), due to the rotation of the earth pushing it off course, shifting (on the south coast) from south to south-west. The strength of the sea breeze depends on the heat of the sun, and whether it is reinforced or opposed by an existing wind. On its own it is unlikely to exceed about Force 4, but it can increase an existing Force 4 off the sea to almost gale strength, which must be borne in mind when sailing off the coast in lovely anticyclonic conditions. By its very nature, however, it does not extend very far from the coast so easier conditions will be found by sailing perhaps five or ten miles offshore. Occasionally in very hot weather, due to the sea cooling down more slowly than the land in the evening, this flow of air is reversed at night to give a **land breeze** (wind off the land). This may be experienced in estuaries, but the air circulation is rarely strong enough to extend the land breeze off the coast.

The Formation of Fog

The heating of the land during the day in fine anticyclonic weather can also give rise to what is known as **radiation fog**. If the skies remain clear at night (which they usually do in these conditions) the hot air is allowed to radiate out into space (clouds acting rather like loft insulation to keep the heat in) and the air close to the ground cools down. The colder air is, the less water vapour it can hold, and this radiation often cools the air to below the temperature at which it can hold the water vapour it already has. This then condenses out into tiny droplets of water, billions and billions of which are what clouds are made of. And fog is cloud at ground level – damp, dismal and extremely difficult to see through.

Radiation fog tends to form in hollows and valleys where the cold air (which is heavier than warm air) collects. When it forms in a river valley it can then roll down the estuary and out to sea for up to five miles, where it remains until the heat of the next day warms up the air sufficiently for it to re-absorb the water vapour, whereupon the fog disappears. Any wind will tend to mix up the layers of warm and cold air, thus speeding up the dissipation of the fog. It generally lifts by late in the morning, although it can linger all day if thick enough, or if any cloud forms to shield it from the sun. Radiation fog is often so low-lying that the sun can be seen shining through it, and a man climbing the mast can sometimes actually see clearly over the top of the fog.

Due to their very localised nature, neither radiation fog nor sea breezes are normally predicted in the shipping forecast, although land forecasts and local radio yachting forecasts are likely to mention them. From what has been said, however, it should be apparent that both can be quite easily predicted by the skipper on the spot (you!), from simple observation in conjunction with the weather forecast.

Sea fog is quite a different matter and will certainly be mentioned in the shipping forecast. This, as its name implies, is formed over the sea by the action of warm moist air passing over colder water. The water cools the air to below its **dew point** (the lowest temperature at which it can hold the water vapour it contains) and the water vapour then condenses out as fog. This type of fog is most common in spring when the water is still cold from the winter (the sea takes a long time to heat up), and depressions bring south-westerly winds that are warm (having come from the tropics) and full of water that they have absorbed from the ocean en route. Sea fog is much more dangerous than radiation fog as it does not burn up with the sun, and is not dispersed by wind; only a complete change of weather conditions will remove it. It can blow easily into adjacent sea areas that have not had it forecast, and appear as from nowhere in odd places where cold water from the depths wells up to the surface due perhaps to strong tidal streams swirling over an uneven bottom. It needs to be treated with great caution.

Frontal fog is basically sea fog that has formed in the warm air around the warm front of a depression. It will lie in a fairly narrow band either side of the front and will pass as the front moves away. It will normally be mentioned in the shipping forecast.

Other Features on the Synoptic Chart

Although the chart is generally dominated by the existence of highs and the passage of lows, there are other features that you will hear mentioned from time to time. **Troughs of low pressure** and **ridges of high pressure** are simply squashed and elongated versions of lows and highs and the weather they give is similar to that of the originals. Ridges, however, can some-times produce cloudy and drizzly weather with poor visibility and often surprisingly strong winds if the isobars are squashed sufficiently close together. A high and a low squeezing against each other can close up the isobars and produce long periods of strong winds where they meet, the anticlockwise winds of the low rein-forcing the clockwise ones of the high. See figure 62. This strong flow of wind, that can remain for days on end if the high is blocking the low and neither moves away, is called an **airstream.**

An **occlusion** (or **occluded front**) is a merging of warm and cold fronts, found near the centre of a low that is **filling** (fizzling out). See figure 65. What happens is that the cold front travels faster than the warm front and gradually catches up with it. It does so nearest the centre of the low first, as the two fronts are closest together here. As the fronts merge so the energy that is causing the low is dissipated and the depression is said to be occluding. The pressure at the centre rises and the isobars drift further apart, whereupon we all breathe a sigh of relief and settle down to some better weather. Or do we?

The wise seaman does not. As the cold front begins to occlude and slow down on catching the warm front its trailing edge

tends to try and overtake it, often forming a kink or wave as it 'trips over itself'. See the bottom left corner of figure 65. This kink, if sufficiently accentuated, can quickly draw a circulation of air around itself and form rapidly into a deep and vicious little low, travelling at great speed in the wake of its dying parent. This **secondary** or **wave depression** will usually have much stronger winds than the original, and can form and travel so fast that it is on you before anyone has time to forecast it. It is invariably the cause of those 'unexpected gales' that wreak havoc in the English Channel from time to time.

The skipper on the spot, however, (you) can forecast it quite easily. Be wary of any occluding depression. When the cold front goes over and the skies clear the barometer will begin rising. Keep a close eye on the sky to the west and on the barometer. Thin wispy high cloud thick-ening from the west and a suddenly falling barometer when you expect it still to be rising are sure signs of an approach-ing wave depression. Winds are likely to be up to two forces stronger than those experienced in the parent depression and the wave will travel perhaps half as fast again. The best place for you, if you can get there in time, is a nice sheltered harbour. Failing that get well out to sea so you have room to heave to and ride it out. See Chapter 9.

Other Types of Forecast

The synoptic chart shown on certain television weather bulletins and pub-lished in daily newspapers is an excellent way of fleshing out the rather meagre details given in the shipping forecast's general synopsis. The latter tends only to give the positions, strengths and move-ments of the major lows and highs, where-as the synoptic chart shows everything – isobars, fronts, occlusions and so on. Regular perusal of these will give you a very good general picture of the weather

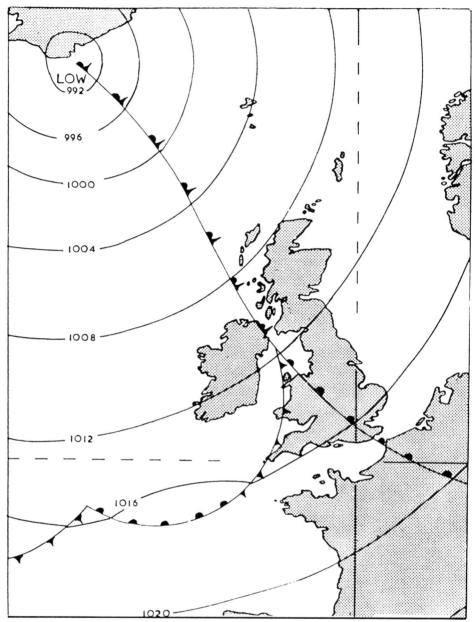

Figure 65

pattern, which will help greatly in your interpretation of the shipping forecast. Bear in mind, however, that it is the general picture, with emphasis on conditions over the land. Use it in conjunction with the shipping forecast, not instead of it. The detailed land forecasts on radio are also most useful, giving much information on the movement and positions of fronts (as they bring rain), about which the shipping forecast seems curiously reticent.

Forecasts more orientated towards the seaman can be had on local radio in yachting areas, by phone from certain Met. Offices and from the Inshore Waters forecast on Radio 4. Details of all these will be found in the Almanac, together with coastguard stations and their phone numbers – from which you can get reports of present weather conditions in their areas (the coastguard will look out of his window and tell you what the weather is doing!). The Inshore Waters Forecast is very good for coastal passages as it concentrates on conditions close inshore. A phone call to a Met. Office can be especially instructive as you can discuss your particular concerns with them, tell them details of your proposed passage and so on, and they will often give a forecast some days ahead. Long range (five day) forecasts can also be obtained on the telephone from British Telecom, and although land-based can be useful for longer range planning. Weather forecasting is moving rapidly into the computer age, and by the time you read this there will likely be many more sources of forecasts available to sailors.

Forecasting the Weather Yourself

Wherever you get forecasts from, never forget the point made at the beginning of this chapter about their fallibility. Having learnt here something of the nature of the weather, you should be able to assess for yourself whether the forecaster's prediction is right or not for where you are. The main points to watch for are the possibility of depressions deepening, altering course or speeding up. The first will bring you stronger winds than forecast; the second will bring conditions forecast for another sea area into your area; and the third will bring you the forecast weather sooner than expected.

You have three basic ways of checking the forecast – your barometer, the look of the sky, and present weather conditions out to the west of you (the normal direction of approach of depressions). You can get the latter from the shipping forecast station reports or from coastguards by phone or radio-telephone (see Appendix 2). Knowing the speed and movement of a depression (from the general synopsis) it is a simple matter to calculate how soon you can expect the present weather at the Scillies to reach, say, the Thames area (check carefully the time for which station reports are issued). You can also compare the actual wind at the Scillies with that forecast and get an idea of whether to expect stronger winds than forecast (or lighter). The barometer movement at the Scillies and other stations in between will help in gauging this. If the wind is forecast for Force 5, for example, and stations to the west of you are reporting Force 7 and barometers falling 'very rapidly' then you should be able to make the obvious deduction. Watch also for the build-up of cloud, the clearing of cloud and so on and tie this in with land forecasts of rain. Remember, the weather almost invariably comes from the west, so look that way to see what is coming.

Do not be a parrot and simply quote the forecast for your sea area. Weigh up *all* the information available to you and make your own assessment. The more you do this, even when not going to sea, the better you will become at it. Listen to the forecasts, look at the television charts, check the actual weather to the west, and watch the sky. Try to build a picture in your mind of the constantly changing synoptic chart and you will soon become adept at interpreting the weather conditions. It will go a long way towards making you a safe and competent skipper as well as providing much interest.

It is a great help to use a pad of **Metmaps** (printed forecast area charts available from chandlers) so that you can keep a record of successive forecasts. You can then look back over them and see how situations have developed. Mark the positions and movements of lows and highs in the synopsis then flesh out details of fronts and isobars etc from station reports, land forecasts and so on to give you as complete a picture as possible. You will have to develop some sort of shorthand to get all the information down as the forecast is often read at frightening speed, especially if it is complicated and only five minutes are available. Or record it on tape and play back at leisure. There is an official system of shorthand symbols but you will probably find it easier to work out your own. Simple abbreviations such as NW (north-west), bec (becoming), v (veering) and so on will be perfectly adequate. Group areas with the same forecast, eg TDFGB (Tyne, Dogger, Fisher, German Bight), and note station reports as Sc-NNE3-6-1015 ↓ s (Scilly Isles – north-north-east Force 3 – visibility 6 miles – barometer reading 1015 millibars, falling slowly). Remember that information is always given in the same order so very concise abbreviations are possible. You will soon get the hang of it.

9

Sailing in Strong Winds

As the wind blows ever stronger so your boat will heel over more and more, until finally the edge of the deck will begin to submerge. This can be very worrying at first, but there is no cause for alarm. Even with the deck half-submerged there will be little risk of a well-designed boat coming to any harm. The more she heels, the more difficult it becomes for the wind to heel her further, because of the increasing righting moment exerted by the keel and by the buoyancy of the hull pressing down on the water. She will, however, begin to sail less and less efficiently, so something needs to be done. What we do is reduce the size of sail area presented to the wind. This will not slow her down, as the increasing wind will produce more power in the sails, but it will diminish the heeling force generated by the wind. She will, in fact, sail faster, as there will be less water resistance with the deck out of the water, and the sails will work more efficiently at the smaller angle of heel. The crew will work better too if the boat is not lying on her ear!

Reefing Sails

The process of reducing sail area is known as **reefing**, and there are two common methods of doing this to a mainsail. One is known as **roller reefing** and consists in principle of simply rolling the mainsail round the boom until sufficient area is left exposed to the wind to drive her efficiently without heeling too much. The other system is known as **slab reefing**, in which the sail is partly lowered, then attached to the ends of the boom at higher points on the luff and the leech, the loose bit in the middle being lashed up so that it does not flap about. With modern slab reefing methods this is not as complicated as it sounds, and the system is often referred to as **jiffy reefing**.

A roller reefing system has a simple winch built in to the tack fitting on the boom. A handle fits into this and can be turned to wind the sail round the boom, the halyard being steadily eased to allow the sail to come down the mast. If there is a gate at the bottom of the track to stop the sliders falling out when the sail is handed, this must be opened to allow the slides out, then closed again on completion of reefing. To get the sail to wind neatly and snugly round the boom some tension should be kept on the halyard, and the end of the boom raised slightly with the topping lift. Many roller reefing booms taper, becoming wider towards the after end, and this takes up more cloth at the leech, thus preventing the boom end from

Photo 42

Slab reefing may sound more trouble-some than this, but is in practice easier, as well as producing a much better shaped sail. The cringles at tack and clew of the mainsail are duplicated further up the sail, usually twice to give two reefs, and lines are led from the boom up through the ones on the leech of the sail then back through a block on the other side of the boom and forward to a cleat. With the weight of the boom taken on the topping lift, the sail is lowered until the **reef cringle** on the luff can be attached to the tack fitting on the boom, and the **reef pendant** through the leech cringle hauled down tight to pull this down to the boom. The **bunt** (middle part) of the sail is then lashed up using small lines sewn into both sides of the sail along the reef line. These are passed under the sail and reef knotted together. Some boats may be fitted with a single line rove through small eyes along the reef line, and this is simply hauled taut to contain the bunt of the sail. Many modern jiffy reefing systems do not bother securing the bunt at all, simply leaving it to dangle. The sail is then reset by tightening the halyard and slackening the topping lift. It is most important with slab reefing to ensure that the strain of the sail is taken by the tack and clew cringles and not by the reef points, which are solely to contain the loose surplus sail. If the foot of the sail runs on an external track on top of the boom the reef points should be tied round only the sail, and not the boom. You can see the layout of the system in figure 66. Both types of reef are shaken out by simply reversing the pro-cesses: take weight of boom on topping lift; slacken halyard; unravel sail; tighten halyard, and slacken topping lift. With roller reefing the sail can be steadily hoisted as it is unrolled from the boom.

Changing Jibs

In order to keep the sailplan balanced after reducing the mainsail in size, we must also reduce the size of the jib. This

drooping. You will generally find that two or three complete rolls round the boom will reduce her heeling noticeably. You must watch the angle of any battens as the reef rolls in; if they are not parallel with the boom they must be removed to pre-vent them breaking or distorting the sail. If the boom vang fits into a slot in the boom this will have to be removed, which is a nuisance as it is particularly valuable in strong winds, both to maintain sail shape and to stop the boom lifting in the air when running or gybing. It can be replaced by attaching it to a length of strong webbing which is rolled round the boom inside the sail, or a special claw-type fitting can be had that clips round the boom, allowing the sail to roll round inside it. Photo 42 shows reefs being taken in by one man who is easing off the halyard as he rolls. The operation is much easier with two people – one for each job.

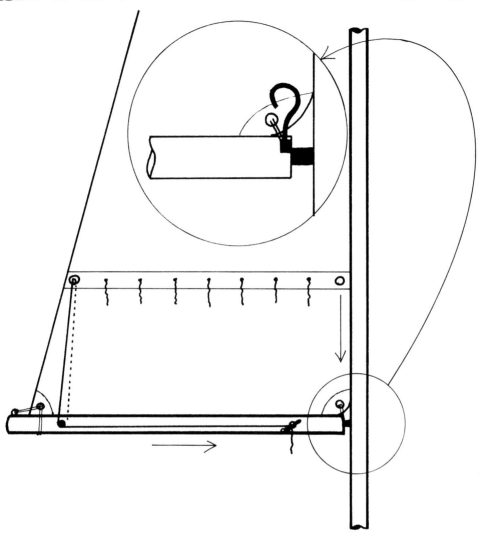

Figure 66

can be done by either changing to a smaller jib or partly furling a suitably-designed **roller-reefing jib**. The latter is a very much simpler operation than the former, consisting simply of slackening off the sheet and hauling in on the furling line until the jib is the required size, then cleating the line and sailing on. It is important here to distinguish between roller-furling jibs and roller-reefing ones; the former being designed to furl only for stowage, while the latter are specially constructed to maintain their shape in the

wind when partly furled. Roller-furling jibs will not set well, and are likely to stretch and be ruined if you sail with them partly furled.

To change a jib you should tie the sailbag containing the smaller jib to something on the foredeck (to stop it blowing away), then lower the jib to the deck. If it is windy it will blow all over the place, and the best way to control it is to sit wedged in the pulpit facing aft and haul the sail down between your legs, gripping it all the while with your knees to control it. Remove the halyard and clip it somewhere safe, then unhank the sail starting from the head, stuffing it gradually head first into a spare bag or down the fo'c'sle hatch as it comes free. Finally remove the tack from the stemhead fitting, but leave the sheets attached. Haul the tack of the new jib from its bag (tack should have been stowed on top) and fix it onto the stemhead fitting, then proceed to hank onto the forestay from the tack upwards. Pull no more sail out of the bag than necessary or it will catch in the wind and blow away! As soon as the clew is uncovered in the bag, take the sheets from the old sail and fit them onto the new one, making sure the foot of the sail is not twisted. When all the sail is hanked onto the stay attach the halyard to the head and hoist the new jib. If you have twin forestays, you can hank the new jib on the spare stay before handing the old one; then drop the old one, change over sheets and halyard, and hoist the new jib before removing and stowing the old one. This is useful when racing as it slows the boat down much less.

Changing jibs can be a wet and uncomfortable business in a rough sea, especially when beating to windward. If you are in no hurry, and have plenty of room to leeward, I would suggest that you run off downwind so that the jib is sheltered by the mainsail, when the operation can be carried out in dry and comfortable conditions, with the boat upright and much steadier.

Heaving To

This is a very handy manoeuvre which holds the boat virtually stopped in the water with the sea on one bow. With the smallest jib set and a deeply reefed mainsail, it is a most comfortable and seamanlike way of riding out a wind that is too strong for you to safely or sensibly sail in. With normal working sails set it enables you to stop for lunch, or to take a good long look at a harbour entrance, and also to reef the mainsail in relatively dry comfort. The process consists simply of

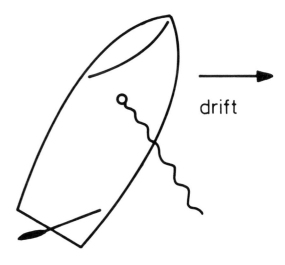

wind

drift

Figure 67

hauling the jib aback, freeing the mainsheet right off, and lashing the tiller to leeward. The jib will tend to blow her head off until some wind fills the mainsail, when the latter (in conjunction with the tiller down to leeward) will tend to push her back into the wind. An equilibrium is soon established with the wind about 70° off the bow and the boat very slowly sailing forward; but with a lot of leeway, so if you heave to in order to ride out bad weather you must have plenty of **sea room** in which you can drift to leeward. The simplest way of heaving to is just to tack and leave the jib sheeted where it is; slacken the mainsheet right off and lash the tiller to leeward. You can see a boat hove-to in figure 67.

If your boat is a traditional heavy type with a long keel, this is exactly what will happen, although you may need to experiment a bit with tiller position, and the mainsail may have to be sheeted in a little in strong winds to stop it flogging. At the opposite extreme, a modern light displacement racer with short fin keel may be quite incapable of heaving to at all, having insufficient directional stability to settle down in any one position. Most modern yachts will fall somewhere between these two stools, and you will have to experiment to find the best way of heaving to, and the direction in which she will then lie. Knowing the principle of working the jib, mainsail and tiller against one another to find an equilibrium position should enable you to understand what is happening. If, in spite of experimentation, your boat will not heave to satisfactorily then I suggest you sell her and buy a proper boat that will. It is a seamanlike ability that all cruising boats should possess.

In very strong winds you may find she lies more comfortably with just the backed jib and no mainsail. She will point downwind and drift much faster to leeward like this, however, so you must be certain of having plenty of safe water to leeward of you.

Steering in Big Waves

Well designed sailing boats tend to need little in the way of special steering techniques as they seem to flow naturally up and down the waves. There are, however, some useful guidelines. When beating to windward you should, in general, aim to luff up slightly over the tops of waves and bear away again down their backs, especially if the waves are steep and tending to stop you. This helps the bow cut through each crest rather than be thumped on the side by it. You should also sail generally slightly further off the wind than you would in calm water, as this will increase speed and give the boat more power to climb over the waves.

Off the wind you must concentrate very hard on steering so that you anticipate the stern being lifted by a wave. When it is, the wave will tend to carry it forward faster than the bow (which slows down in the trough) and thus swing the boat round towards the wind. This needs to be corrected for just before it happens, as the

water in the wavecrest will then be stationary in relation to the rudder, and the rudder will not work. This behaviour is called **broaching.**

Running Downwind

Strong winds make themselves felt in no uncertain manner when you are beating to windward, and it is easy enough to recognise the time to reduce sail. When running or broad reaching, however, conditions can feel quite comfortable onboard long after they have actually become dangerous. There are two dangers to consider. The first is the possibility of having to suddenly round up hard on the wind; to pick up a man overboard perhaps (see Chapter 11). The second is of broaching, which in big waves can cause the boat to be thrown right on her side and possibly swamped by the next wave. The simple rule when sailing downwind in a blow is never to carry more sail than you would want for beating in that wind. You will then be in a position to manoeuvre to windward immediately in an emergency; added to which this amount of sail will give you a comfortable, steady ride, and will probably automatically cause you to sail slowly enough to avoid the possibility of broaching.

The danger from broaching comes basically from sailing too fast. The nearer your speed is to that of the waves, the longer will the stern sit on the front of each crest (during which time there will be little water flow past the rudder), and the greater the likelihood of the wave broaching you as the bow slows down in the trough. The risk can be reduced, and steering made easier, by carrying the bulk of your sail area for'ard, so that the bow tends to be pushed downwind all the time rather than the stern. In very strong winds you should run with just a small jib and no mainsail. In howling gales bare poles (mast and rigging alone) may drive you quite fast enough for comfort and safety.

Broaching can also occur without the

assistance of waves, if the boat rolls violently while running. The constant changing of hull shape in the water and sailplan presented to the wind creates considerable instability, and you could find the boat suddenly broaching to weather or crash-gybing round to leeward. This rolling is generally caused by carrying spinnakers and suchlike on a short-keeled boat in too much wind, but can equally result from letting the mainsail out so far that the top of it projects ahead of the mast. The likelihood of this is reduced greatly by the use of a tight boom vang to stop the boom lifting and allowing the head of the sail to go forward. The risk of an unexpected gybe, usually through inattentive steering, can be reduced by rigging a **preventer**. This is a strong warp

led from the end of the boom and secured somewhere right for'ard. It should be rigged with the mainsail eased right out, so that it comes very tight when the main is hauled into its correct position. If the boat accidentally gybes, it will stop the boom crashing across. Another method is to wrap a canvas strop round the boom above the gunwhale and haul down tightly on this with a small tackle shackled to the jibsheet track. However, if you do gybe with a preventer rigged, you may not find it possible to steer her back to the original course because of the wind pressure on the 'backed' mainsail. Thus the first type of preventer is best, if it has a very long tail, as it can then be gradually eased off to allow the boom to gybe slowly and gently.

Figure 68 The water flowing forward at the top of the wave is what causes broaching. Partly this is because that water pushes the stern forward while the flow in the trough is holding the bow back; and partly it is because the rudder is sat in water that is moving forward at roughly the same speed as it. Thus the rudder will not steer, as it needs a backward flow of water past it that it can deflect to one side of the stern.

Running for Shelter

It is very tempting to run for the haven of a sheltered harbour when bad weather is forecast, but this is a decision that must be made with great care. There are many dangers involved in running down to a lee shore for shelter, whereas most modern cruisers (handled properly) can safely, if

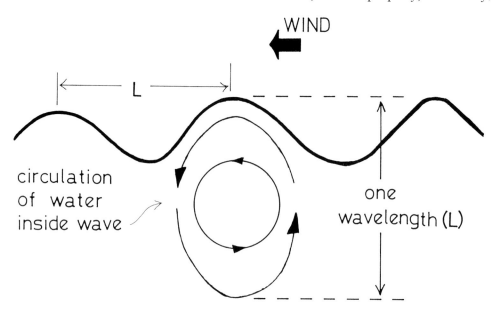

WIND

L

circulation of water inside wave

one wavelength (L)

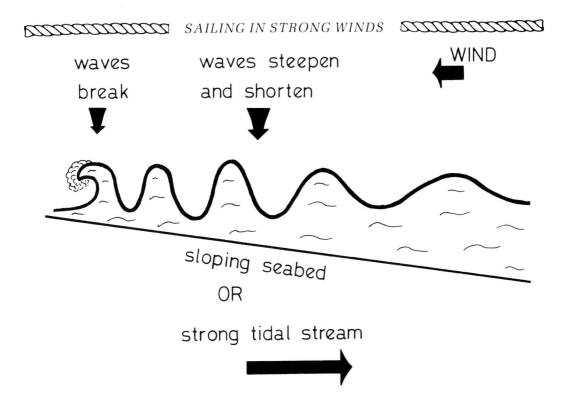

waves break

waves steepen and shorten

WIND

sloping seabed

OR

strong tidal stream

Figure 69

uncomfortably, ride out at sea all but the severest of gales. The two main dangers of running inshore are: missing the harbour and being unable to beat back out to sea against the gale; and the fact that waves are more dangerous in the shallow water close to land than they are in the open sea. The reason for the latter is that the energy of a wave reaches down below the surface a distance equal to the length between crests. This energy causes water to circulate inside the wave (see figure 68) and if the depth decreases to near the wavelength, the water at the bottom of the wave drags and slows down. This causes the wave to grow higher and steeper as the top of it tries to overtake the bottom. The same thing occurs when the waves are running against the tidal stream, and you can see the result in figure 69. Eventually the wave breaks, and this type of steep, breaking wave can overwhelm and sink a small boat. If tidal streams converge from different directions, as they might off a

headland, these breaking waves will run all ways, causing confused seas that can throw a small cruiser around like a cork. In a gale of wind she would be lucky not to break up and founder. Even if the water is deep inshore, steep cliffs and seawalls cause waves to rebound and run out against the incoming ones, causing rough and confused seas.

Thus in bad weather you should keep well clear of strong tidal streams (off headlands etc) and shallow water, and the best place to do this is well out to sea; reefed down or hove to. Running for shelter should only be attempted if you are absolutely certain you can get safely into harbour before the gale strikes, or if the harbour lies round a corner so that you can safely run well clear of the headland then round up gradually into wide sheltered waters. It must also be sheltered from any possible windshift (sou'west gale veering to a nor'west gale, for example), and ideally you should have a second harbour lined up further to leeward in case you miss the first. Navigation is more difficult in bad weather, so this is quite likely. More boats are lost running for shelter than ever are out at sea, so it is not a decision to be taken lightly. If you are not capable and confident of riding out bad weather you should not be at sea.

Handling Rough Weather

It is important not to let rough weather intimidate you. It can be frightening and tiring and uncomfortable, but if you have a well-found boat and know what you are doing it is rarely dangerous. It can be, however, if you let it get the better of you. Face it and do all the things you know must be done: reefing, sail-changing, secure lashing of all gear and hatches and so on. Do all this *before* the weather gets unmanageable as it will be a lot easier; then get a good meal inside yourselves, and put on warm, dry clothes and water-proofs. You will then not only be ready for it, but will feel ready for it. Remember that gales do not blow forever; usually the worse they are the faster they pass by. If rough seas are caused by the wind blow-ing against the tide, you can take comfort from the fact that they will last only six hours, until the tide turns with the wind.

Seasickness

This is not a music hall joke, but a very important consideration in bad weather. Its effect on people varies from mild queasiness, through a longing to die, to total mental and physical incapacitation. The last can clearly be very serious in a small crew; disastrous if it strikes skipper or navigator. Even partial seasickness, especially if combined with tiredness, can drastically affect the ability of a skipper to make decisions, and a navigator to pro-duce accurate calculations. There are various commercial remedies available, ranging from pills which can make you so drowsy that you might as well have stayed at home in bed, to an elastic band that applies acupressure to a point on the wrist, the latter being favourably reported on and without side effects.

There is, however, a great deal that you can do yourself to prevent seasickness. Basically it is caused by the balancing mechanism of the inner ear being unable to cope with your constant movement. This unsettled feeling is communicated to the stomach which then reacts accord-ingly. The more settled the stomach is, the less likely it is to regurgitate its contents, and there are two basic things that un-settle the stomach – tension (from appre-hension); and lack of simple solid food. If you keep busy so that you have no time to think about being sick, and feed well both before sailing and while sailing, you will go a long way to preventing seasickness. Anything that might sit uneasily in the stomach should be avoided. Greasy foods, too much liquid (especially tea), and hangovers are worst. Porridge, scrambled egg, dry bread and biscuits, soups, stews, cocoa and suchlike are best. And keep on deck in the fresh air; the atmosphere down below in rough weather is very conducive to seasickness.

The onset of seasickness is accom-panied by a feeling of lethargy, and a disinclination to eat. Both must be fought. Take over the steering so that you keep occupied and busy, and force food into yourself. Do not dwell on the motion by starting at the mast waving across the sky as this will confuse the inner ear even more. The sense of motion can be reduced considerably by ensuring that all loose gear is stowed securely. The sound of things crashing and rattling around, and the sight of them swinging about will not help your inner ear to settle down. Even the sight of a wooden spoon swinging in the galley can bring on sickness. Wedge yourself so that you move with the boat, rather than sway about trying to keep upright like the Hollywood sailor. The former is both less tiring and less likely to bring on sickness. Breathe deeply and slowly of the fresh air, relax, and take control of the situation.

10
Making a Coastal Passage

Navigation is the business of finding your way from one place to another on the sea. It can be a complex mixture of art and science, requiring considerable training and experience to carry out competently and reliably. For a short coastal passage in fair weather, however, the knowledge required is fairly simple. If you extend your cruising to pastures further afield, you must then study more specialised books on the subject (see Appendix 3). Let us first consider the equipment that we need for making a coastal passage.

Navigation Equipment

The first requirement is suitable charts to cover the passage. There are two types of chart – large scale detailed ones for getting in and out of harbours, and small scale ones covering the passage (if possible with both harbours on the same chart). These charts can be chosen from a **Chart Atlas** at the Chart Agents: a large booklet showing the outlines of the areas covered by each chart, together with a chart reference number. This number will be found clearly marked in the corners of the actual chart, in bold type just on the outside of the border.

Charts have to be corrected regularly to allow for changes to depths, buoys and so on, and the corrections are noted at the bottom of the chart; each year being followed by the number of the correction. If you buy charts from a proper agent they will be corrected to date, and you should return them to him each winter for updating. Out-of-date charts can be highly dangerous, for obvious reasons. When you are experienced you can, if you wish, obtain the corrections from the Chart Agent and do them yourself. It is not difficult.

A **Pilot Book** giving detailed navigational information for the area in which we are sailing, and a **Nautical Almanac**, containing vast amounts of useful information such as tide tables and so on (see Appendix 3) are essential items. Although some Almanacs carry potted chartlets and information on many harbours, these should only be used for general planning; they are no substitute for proper Pilot Books and charts. Both these publications need updating annually. A **Tidal Stream Atlas**, showing rates and directions of tidal streams in the area, is very useful; although small, less accurate versions are contained in the Almanac. To these books and charts we must add pencils (half a dozen soft 2B), pencil sharpener, soft rubber, dividers (for measuring distances – the single-handed type as shown are

Photo 43

easiest to use), compasses (for drawing curves and marking off distances), a parallel ruler (for transferring bearings and position lines on the chart), a small notebook and a ship's **logbook** for noting down navigational information while on passage. See photo 43.

In the cockpit we should have a **steering compass** for steering by, a small **hand-bearing compass** for taking bearings of landmarks, etc, a **log** for measuring the distance we sail through the water, a pair of binoculars to help us identify objects at a distance, and either a leadline or an echo-sounder (or both) for measuring the depth of the water. The log may be fitted into the hull or towed astern on a line. Binoculars should be the type described as 7×50, having 7× magnification and large 50mm lenses to gather maximum light for visibility at dawn and dusk. Anything more powerful than 7× will be very difficult to hold steady without blur-

ring the image, although the popular birdwatcher's 8×30 is usable, if less efficient than the traditional seaman's 7×50. If you have an echo-sounder (which you will find most useful), you should also carry a leadline in case of breakdown, and also for sounding right for'ard or from the dinghy.

The steering compass shows us the direction of Magnetic North, which is slightly to one side of True North (the North Pole), so enabling us to know in what direction the boat is pointing. Essentially it consists of a card stuck on top of a pivoting magnet, usually marked round the circumference in degrees from 000° (North) through 090° (East), 180° (South), 270° (West) to 360° (North again), although some old compasses are marked in **points** as in the compass rose in Chapter 8. A line at the front of the compass (called the **lubber's line**) shows the direction in which the boat is pointing. See photo 44. A handbearing compass is a small version of this that can be held in the hand. A 'gunsight' at the front can be lined up with an object and its bearing read off from the compass card.

The magnet in a compass is easily affected by the proximity of steel, electronic equipment or other magnets, and it is most important that such things as beer cans, cameras, light-meters, knives, radios, electronic equipment and suchlike are kept at least three feet from the compass. Any permanent influences in the boat, such as engine, rigging etc, will affect the compass at greater distances and their effects must be corrected for by adjusting the compass with small magnets fixed around it. This process is known as **swinging the compass**, and most harbours have a **compass adjuster** (often the Harbourmaster) who will check the compass on all its headings, then fix the magnets around it to reduce errors to a

Photo 44 It is important when viewing the compass to do so from a position where the lubber's line aligns with the bow, or you will get a false reading. Generally it is best to steer on a landmark, or star at night, with occasional glances at the compass to confirm the course. Staring constantly at the compass is extremely tiring, especially at night.

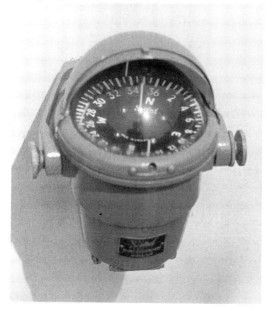

minimum. The remaining errors, which will vary with the direction in which the boat is pointing (her **heading**), are known as **Deviation**, and they will be listed on a card called a **Deviation Card** (see figure 70) which should be kept by the chart table. The errors can then be allowed for when plotting a course to steer by the compass, as we shall discuss later in this chapter. The compass should be swung every other year, unless it is removed from the boat or any major work is done on the boat, when it should be swung before going to sea again in case the Deviation has altered. The residual magnetism in the boat that causes Deviation is partly influenced by the Earth's magnetic field, and if a boat sits pointing in the same direction for about six months this field can alter her magnetic pattern, and so the Deviation. The handbearing compass cannot be corrected like this, so it must always be used in a part of the boat as far as possible from metal, electronics etc. In such a position it can be aligned with the centreline to give a rough check on the accuracy of the steering compass.

Planning the Passage

Let us imagine we want to sail down the coast of East Anglia from Great Yarmouth to the small harbour of Southwold, a straight line passage of some seventeen miles. This may not seem very far, but in the quiet conditions that you should pick for your first coastal passage it will probably take most of the daylight hours by the time you have negotiated your way in and out of the harbours and moored up. The first step is to purchase the necessary large and small scale charts to cover this passage, and make sure you have a Pilot Book for the area and a Nautical Almanac for the current year. Carefully read all the information that the Pilot gives on both harbours and the coastline between them. Do not bother too much with details at this stage; just concentrate on gaining a general picture of the passage and its

DEVIATION CARD Steering compass

Yacht ___ *THISTLE*

Date ___ *8th May 1988*

Magnetic course	Deviation	Compass course
000	2W	002
015	2W	017
030	3W	033
045	3W	048
060	4W	064
075	3W	078
090	3W	093
105	3W	108
120	2W	122
135	1W	136
150	1W	151
165	1W	166
180	0	180
195	0	195
210	0	210
225	0	225
240	1E	239
255	2E	253
270	2E	268
285	3E	282
300	2E	298
315	1E	314
330	0	330
345	1W	346
360	2W	002

Figure 70 The right-hand column shows the courses to steer by the compass in order to make good the magnetic courses in the left-hand column.

problems. Then spread out the charts and peruse them closely, watching out for the things mentioned in the Pilot.

There is quite a lot to planning even a short passage like this, and you will find it beneficial to consider it in three separate stages: getting out of Yarmouth and into a suitable position from which course can be set to Southwold; the actual coastal passage from this point to a similar point off Southwold; then the approach and entry to Southwold harbour itself, including the business of finding somewhere to berth. In terms of these stages two main points come to light from the initial chart and Pilot information. The first is that although Southwold and Yarmouth are, navigationally speaking, simple harbours to negotiate, having clear water with no dangers, they both have long narrow entrances and thus experience very strong tidal streams at times. These can make it difficult, dangerous or even impossible in a small boat to manoeuvre through the entrances at certain stages of the tide, so the timing of these sections of the passage is most important. This business of timing passages to get maximum benefit from tidal streams and so on is a crucial aspect of coastal sailing, and the reasons will emerge in more detail as we proceed. Yarmouth is also a very busy commercial harbour (full details in the Pilot), so care will have to be taken to keep clear of large ships, especially when a strong tide makes everyone's manoeuvring particularly difficult.

The other immediately obvious problem is the plethora of shallow and dangerous sandbanks between Yarmouth and Lowestoft, as you can see on the section of passage chart in figure 71. Although the initial stage of the trip will be well inshore of them, you can see from the chart that there is a slightly tricky bit through the banks as we pass Lowestoft. Thus this passage needs to be taken as four stages – out of Yarmouth and down to Lowestoft; through the banks off Lowestoft; thence to a point off Southwold; and finally into Southwold Harbour. Let us look in detail at these stages.

Leaving Yarmouth

The timing of departure from Yarmouth must take into account not only the tidal streams in the harbour and entrance as we leave, but also those along the coast down to Southwold, and those in the harbour when on arrival. Ideally we want to leave Yarmouth at a favourable time, sail down the coast with a fair tide, negotiate any tricky bits off Lowestoft with either slack or favourable streams, and enter South-wold at the best time recommended by the Pilot. This, of course, will very often be a pipedream, and some sort of compromise usually has to be made; the least danger-ous aspects of the timing being the ones to compromise – most likely the fair tide down the coast. We may also have to be prepared to hang about hove to off South-wold waiting for a suitable time to enter. A sailing boat is not a motorcar, and it is rare that a passage can simply be made straight from one place to another at a time suitable to ourselves! I cannot stress too strongly the importance of timing tides; it is not uncommon for a place to be negotiable in perfect safety and comfort at one stage of the tide, and half an hour later to be a death trap for a small boat. See Chapter 9.

Both Yarmouth and Southwold experi-ence ebb streams of up to six knots at springs, and streams of this strength can be highly dangerous for small boats, even under power. Whether the stream is with or against the boat's progress, the slightest misjudgement of steering in such a con-fined space can cause all control of the boat to be lost. Thus exit and entry should be made near slack High Water, when weak streams combine with the maximum width of channel to make manoeuvring easiest. According to the Pilot the ebb does not begin running out of Yarmouth until 1½ hours after High Water, and one hour later the stream along the coast begins running to the North. We can find this either from a Tidal Stream Atlas or from the **tidal diamonds** on the chart: there is one just off Yarmouth with a J inside it; one off Lowestoft marked N; and one off Southwold marked S. Details of direction and rates of the streams (at both

neaps and springs) are listed at the top left of the chart for the positions of all the diamonds on it. You will discover that tidal information is frequently calculated from the time of High Water at Dover, and these Dover tide times will be found in the Almanac (often on a loose card for easy reference). You can see that if we leave Yarmouth at High Water, as recom-mended, we will have some six hours of foul tide against us as we sail down the coast. The first four hours of it are shown in the tidal stream atlases in figure 72.

However, the width of the channel is not reduced at Low Water (as you can see from the soundings on the chart of Yar-mouth entrance in figure 73 – deep water extends to the banks), so it would make sense to leave on the last of the ebb, which is about two hours after Low Water. The Almanac tells us that this coincides with six hours after High Water Dover, and if we refer to the information on tidal dia-mond J for that time, we find that the ebb stream will carry us out of Yarmouth just as the flood is beginning to run south down the coast. This sounds ideal, but how does it place us for passing Lowestoft? The distance is about six miles, and with a fair tide under us we should cover that (given a reasonable wind) in little over an hour. A check of tidal diamond N (close off Lowestoft) shows that the stream will be running at nearly two knots by the time we get there. With the shallow patches, banks and channels in the area, the stream will undoubtedly be both accelerated and deflected in places, and in strong winds against the tide it will be very rough, with steep, uneven, breaking seas. See the

overleaf
Figure 71 The dark areas show the shallow banks – look for the soundings and drying heights, and note the CAUTION marked on the land between Yarmouth and Lowestoft. The difficult shallows off Lowestoft will be seen more clearly on the larger scale chart in figure 74.

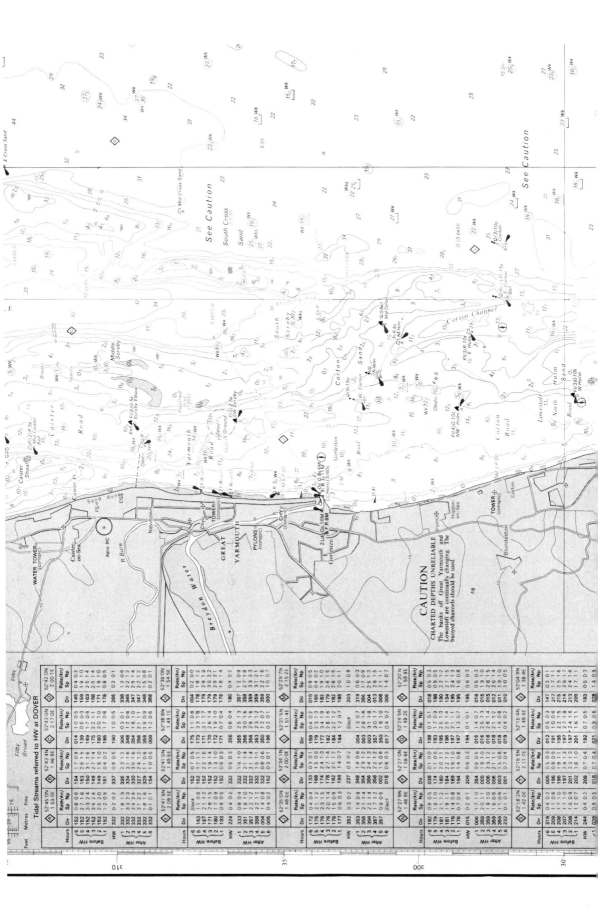

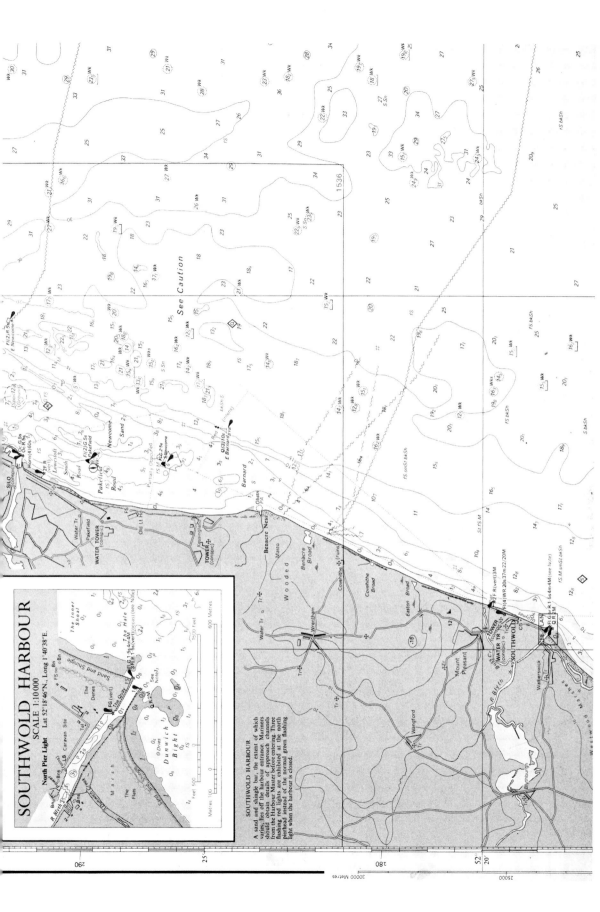

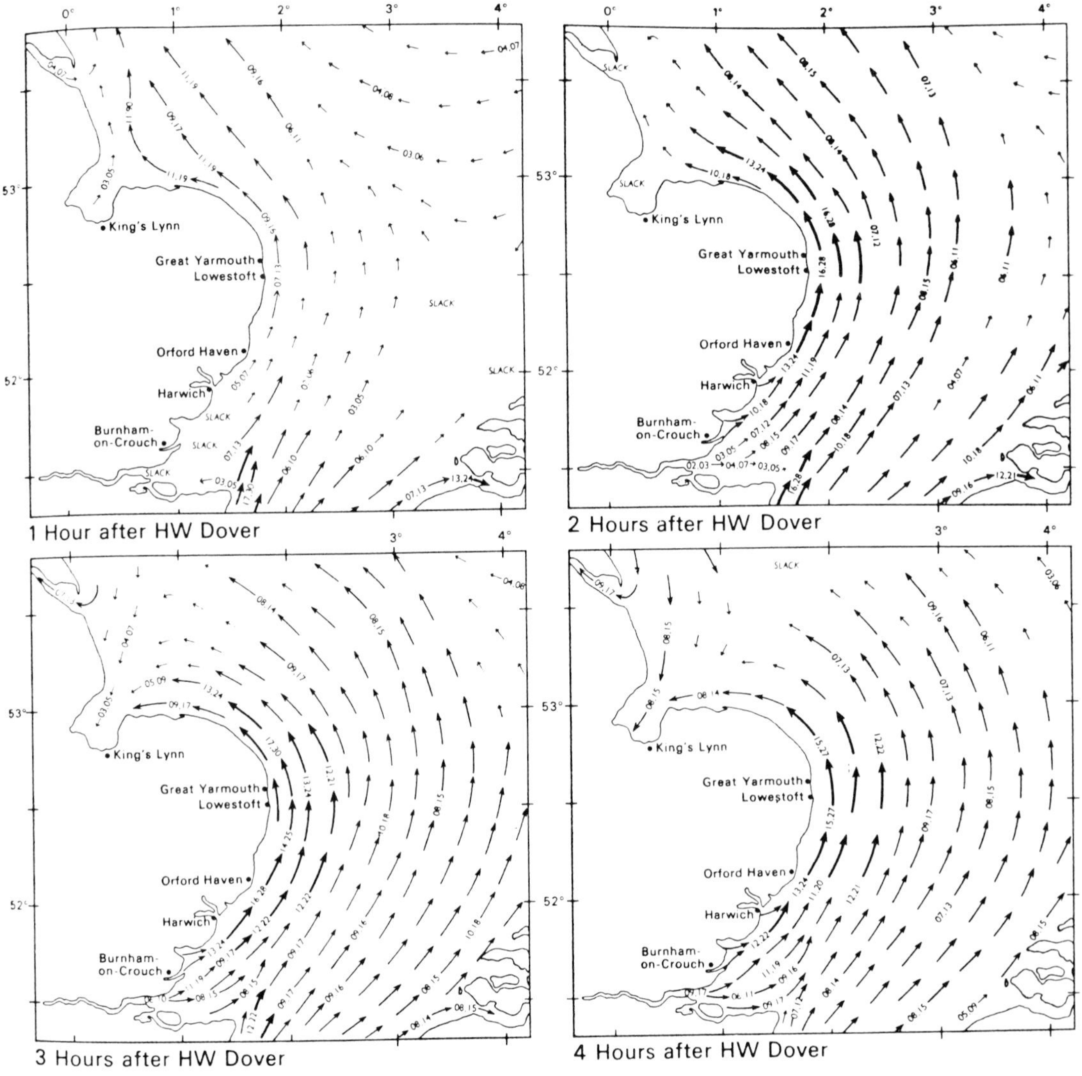
1 Hour after HW Dover
2 Hours after HW Dover
3 Hours after HW Dover
4 Hours after HW Dover
0°
1°
2°
3°
4°
53°
52°
King's Lynn
Great Yarmouth
Lowestoft
Orford Haven
Harwich
Burnham-on-Crouch
SLACK

Figure 72

larger scale chart of 'Approaches to Lowestoft' in figure 74. In quiet conditions, which you should certainly choose for a first passage, there may be a bit of a popple if the tides are on springs, but otherwise the stream will simply speed you on your way. In areas like this it is wise to limit cruises to the slacker neap tides until you gain experience.

Passing Lowestoft

The East Coast Pilot tells us that the best way past Lowestoft is close inshore, where there is a clear channel marked by buoys. The two just off Lowestoft in figure 74 lead us into it, and you can see the line of buoys in figure 71 leading away down to the south. These buoys come in a variety of shapes and colours, which tell us in which direction the danger they are marking lies from them. There are two basic groups of buoys – **Lateral** buoys which simply mark the edges of channels;

and **Cardinal** buoys which are posted in particular directions from isolated dangers. There are three types of lateral buoy, each with its own shape and colour. **Starboard-hand** buoys are green and conical, and mark the starboard sides of channels as viewed when proceeding in the direction of the main flood stream. To avoid confusion this direction is clearly marked on charts, shown by the wide open arrowheads with small circles either side of their tips that you can see at the bottom left and top middle of figure 74. On the charts these buoys are shown as solid black cones with the letter G underneath. **Port-hand** buoys are red and can-shaped, and mark the port side of a channel. They are shown as open cans on the chart, with R underneath. When sailing in the direction of the flood stream they should be left as their names imply – on your port side or your starboard side. When sailing in the opposite direction, of course, they are left the other way round. See photos 45 and 46. **Middle ground** buoys are not so often encountered: they are spherical with horizontal bands of red and white or green and white, and they mark the ends of a bank around which navigable channels flow both sides. The colouring indicates the main channel, a green and white one being treated as a starboard-hand buoy if you want to take the main channel.

Cardinal buoyage is rather more complex than this, as you can see in figure 75. There are four types, and they are positioned as shown – to the north, south, east and west of dangers. They have varying combinations of yellow and black bands, and different **topmarks**, as you can see. They are much taller and narrower than Lateral marks, and are generally visible at greater distances. In many places, especially small creeks and harbours, channels and dangers may be marked in different ways, as you can see in figure 76.

Most of these buoys have lights that flash in a variety of ways to make them easily identifiable at night, and you will find details in the Almanac. Those with lights have little blobs sticking out from them on the chart. Buoys can also move, especially if they are offshore in rough water and strong tides, and generally should not be implicitly relied upon for navigation. Those close to commercial harbours, however, will be watched and maintained closely, so will be fairly reliable. Ideally, your position should always be checked from fixed marks on the shore, as we shall see later, and buoys then used as a general guide to progress.

Entering Southwold

You can see a small chart of Southwold Harbour inset on the left side of the passage chart in figure 71. This is a similar long narrow entrance to Yarmouth, but with the important difference that there is a lot of shallow water about, as you can see from the dark sections marked with drying heights. The width of this harbour is reduced considerably as the tide falls, so it will benefit us to enter near High Water when we will have more room to

overleaf
Figure 73 Note all the information on this chart – reference number, title, depths, tidal levels etc, and the warning about **shoaling** in the harbour entrance. The scales round the edges are part of a world-wide position grid system, by which the position of anything at sea can be noted. The vertical scale up the left-hand side is called **Latitude** and is measured in degrees and minutes (60′ in a degree) from the equator (0°) to the North and South Poles (90° North and 90° South). The line across the right-hand plan is 52°35′ North, and you can see from the size of the minutes on the plans and on the outside of the main chart that the plans are a much larger scale. The horizontal measurements along the top are called **Longitude**, and this is measured East and West of Greenwich (in London). You can see at the top of Plan A that Yarmouth is 1°44′ East of Greenwich (as the harbour goes further west in Plan B, so the Longitude decreases). Thus we can say that the position of Yarmouth is about 52°35′N and 01°44′E.

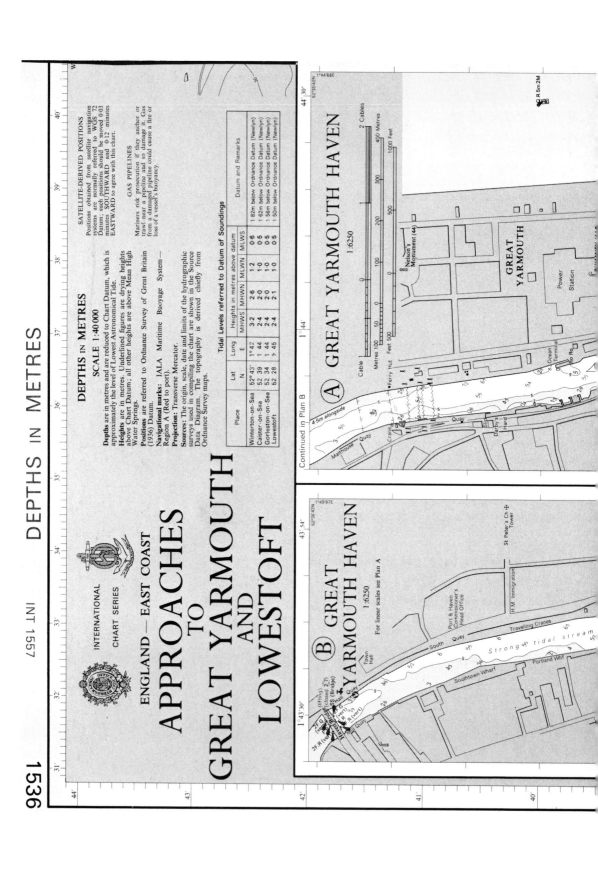

ENGLAND — EAST COAST

APPROACHES
TO
GREAT YARMOUTH
AND
LOWESTOFT

INTERNATIONAL CHART SERIES

DEPTHS IN METRES

SCALE 1:40000

Depths are in metres and are reduced to Chart Datum, which is approximately the level of Lowest Astronomical Tide.

Heights are in metres. Underlined figures are drying heights above Chart Datum; all other heights are above Mean High Water Springs.

Positions are referred to Ordnance Survey of Great Britain (1936) Datum.

Navigational marks: IALA Maritime Buoyage System— Region A (Red to port).

Projection: Transverse Mercator.

Sources: The origin, scale, date and limits of the hydrographic surveys used in compiling the chart are shown in the Source Data Diagram. The topography is derived chiefly from Ordnance Survey maps.

SATELLITE-DERIVED POSITIONS

Positions obtained from satellite navigation systems are normally referred to WGS 72 Datum; such positions should be moved 0·03 minutes SOUTHWARD and 0·12 minutes EASTWARD to agree with this chart.

GAS PIPELINES

Mariners risk prosecution if they anchor or trawl near a pipeline and so damage it. Gas from a damaged pipeline could cause a fire or loss of a vessel's buoyancy.

Tidal Levels referred to Datum of Soundings

Place	Lat N	Long E	Heights in metres above datum				Datum and Remarks
			MHWS	MHWN	MLWN	MLWS	
Winterton-on-Sea	52°43′	1°42′	3·2	2·6	1·2	0·6	1·82m below Ordnance Datum (Newlyn)
Caister-on-Sea	52 39	1 44	2·4	2·0	1·0	0·5	1·82m below Ordnance Datum (Newlyn)
Gorleston-on-Sea	52 34	1 44	2·4	2·0	1·0	0·5	1·56m below Ordnance Datum (Newlyn)
Lowestoft	52 28	1 45	2·4	2·1	1·0	0·5	1·50m below Ordnance Datum (Newlyn)

Ⓐ GREAT YARMOUTH HAVEN
1:6250

GREAT YARMOUTH

Nelson's Monument (44)

Power Station

Cable   Ferry Hut   Ocean Terminal   Ro Ro

Malthouse Quay   Crane   4·5m alongside   Quay   Derby's Hard

Continued in Plan B

Ⓑ GREAT YARMOUTH HAVEN
1:6250

For linear scales see Plan A

St Peter's Ch Tower

Town Hall   Port & Haven Commissioner's Head Office   H.M. Immigration

South   Quay   Travelling Cranes

Strong tidal stream

Southtown Wharf   Portland Whf

Town Hall Quay   Hall Quay

2F·R(vert)

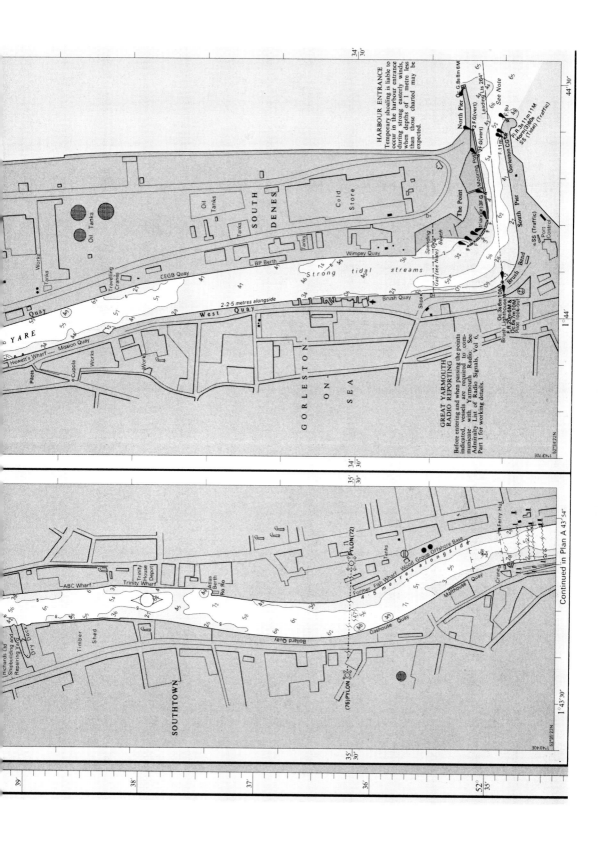

HARBOUR ENTRANCE

Temporary shoaling is liable to occur in the harbour entrance during strong easterly winds, when depths of 1 metre less than those charted may be expected.

GREAT YARMOUTH
RADIO REPORTING

Before entering and when passing the points indicated, vessels are required to communicate with Yarmouth Radio. See Admiralty List of Radio Signals, Vol 6, Part 1 for working details.

SOUTH DENES

Oil Tanks
Tanks
Oil Tanks
Cold Store
Tanks
Wimpey Quay
BP Berth
CEGB Quay
Travelling Cranes
Quay
Tanks
Works

Strong tidal streams
Spending Beach
Gas (see Note)
The Point
North Pier Oc G 8s 8M 6M
2 F (vert)
Mooring Post
2F G(vert)
Leading lts 266°
See Note
Triangle 3F G
Gorleston CG Stn
F 11m
F.Bu
Brush Bend
South Pier
Port Control
SS (Traffic)
Brush Lighthouse
Oc.3s 6m 12M
F.R.20m 6M &
Oc.6s 7m 10M
Pilot 1055.000?
F.R.3s 11m 11M
Horn(3)60s
SS (Tidal) (Traffic)

YARE
Hewett's Wharf
Mission Quay
Pilots
Cupola
Works
Works
West Quay
2·2·5 metres alongside
Brush Quay
Silos

GORLESTON-
ON-
SEA

Continued in Plan A 43'54"

SOUTHTOWN

Richards Ltd
Shipbuilding and
Repairing Yard
Dry Dock
Timber Shed
ABC Wharf
Trinity House Depot
Trinity Wharf
Atlas Berth
Ro Ro
(76)PYLON
(72)PYLON
Tanks
Former Fish Wharf
Wood Group Offshore Base
4·5 metres alongside
Bollard Quay
Gashouse Quay
Malthouse Quay
Cranes
Ferry Hut

SOUTHTOWN

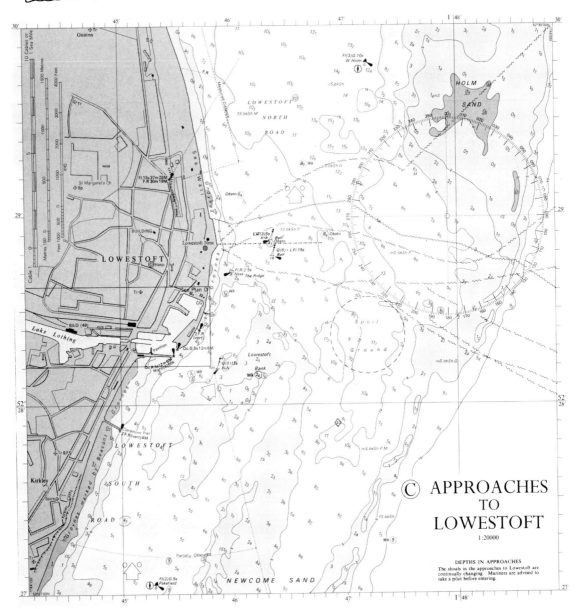

Figure 74 Distances on a chart are measured from the Latitude scale at the side – one minute of latitude being equal to a nautical mile. These distances must always be measured at approximately the same Latitude at which they will be plotted, as the actual length on the chart of a minute of Latitude varies, growing longer as you go further north. This is because the chart is a slightly distorted version of the actual Earth's surface, due to the way it is printed. On large scale charts like this one there is often also a distance scale, as you can see at the top left. Note the churches, lighthouses etc on the land that can be used for fixing your position – see figure 77.

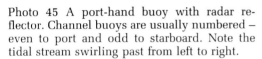

Photo 45 A port-hand buoy with radar reflector. Channel buoys are usually numbered – even to port and odd to starboard. Note the tidal stream swirling past from left to right.

Photo 46 A starboard-hand buoy. The lattice work reduces wind resistance but the shape is quite clear from a distance.

manoeuvre. The Pilot warns of very strong tides, especially on the ebb (when reinforced by river water running out), so the best time to enter would seem to be on the last of the flood. With a passage time of roughly four hours from outside Yarmouth Harbour (which we left on the last of the ebb) we should arrive off Southwold about half flood Yarmouth. The Almanac tells us that High Water Southwold is roughly an hour later than at Yarmouth, so we should be arriving about four hours before High Water. This is a bit earlier than we would like to enter, but it suits well as it gives spare time to allow for delays, light winds and so on. We can take our time and sail up to the harbour for a good look, then stand off again while

we plan the details of entering. When doing this we should keep uptide of the harbour so that we do not have to flog against a foul tide to get back to it. If the tides are neap we can probably safely enter shortly after half flood, but at spring tides we would be better to wait till the stream slackens off nearer High Water. Detailed information on entering will be found in the Pilot.

Making the Passage

In fair weather there are no great navigational difficulties about this passage, the working of the tides being the important factor – as it so often is in coastal sailing. Some harbours will, of course, be

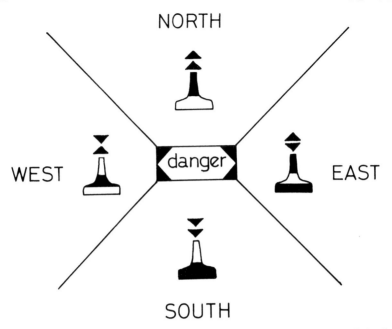

NORTH

WEST　danger　EAST

SOUTH

Figure 75 Note that the North cardinal is *north of* the danger. Many people get confused and think the danger is to the north. The way to remember them is to visualise north UP the page and south DOWN it; west written IN towards the middle and east written OUT towards the edge. Thus the north cardinal buoy has both topmarks pointing UP and the black band UP at the top, while the south has them both pointing DOWN and the black band DOWN at the bottom. The west cardinal has the topmarks pointing IN towards each other and the black band IN the middle, while the east has topmarks pointing OUT from each other and black bands on the OUTside of the middle.

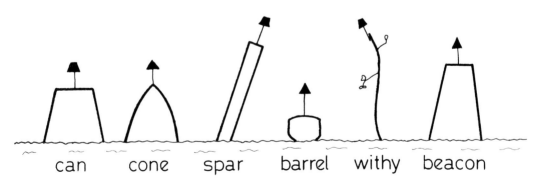

can　　cone　　spar　　barrel　withy　beacon

Figure 76

more difficult to enter and leave than these two, but experience and further reading (Pilots, Almanac and specialist navigation books) will all help develop the necessary confidence and ability. It is important to build these up with short and simple trips in good weather before you go charging off into the wild blue yonder, or you could suddenly find yourself, perhaps literally out of your depth. The sea can be a frightening and dangerous place at such times.

Good preparation is the keynote of a safe passage, and we have already made a lot of ours. We have carefully checked through the route on charts and in the Pilot, selected the best way through the tricky bits, decided on the most favourable time to both leave and arrive, and should have a good picture in our minds of what we are about to undertake. It only remains to choose a day when both tidal conditions and weather are suitable, and we are ready to go.

Leaving Yarmouth is a simple matter of following the harbour out to sea, keeping on the starboard side of the channel and watching out for big ships on the move. If you have VHF radio you can call the harbourmaster before leaving to tell him your intentions and ask about shipping movements. If there is a coastguard station along your route, you can call him for a weather report and also to inform him of your passage – he will then keep an eye open for you. If you have no VHF, use the telephone ashore. Details of all this, and phone numbers, will be in the Almanac. The coastguard service runs a system whereby you can register with them information about your boat, and who to contact in emergency, so if you become overdue they know who to inform

Figure 77 The best type of fix is three intersecting bearings of shore objects, taken with the hand-bearing compass and plotted on the chart as shown (see figure 79). They should be taken as rapidly as possible, and ideally at 60° to one another. If the objects are close together, slight errors in the bearings will be magnified by the time they cross, and a large triangle (known as a cocked hat) will ensue. A small cocked hat is normal, and your position should be taken as the corner nearest to danger. A large **cocked hat** shows an error: check you have plotted the bearings from the correct objects! Write the time and log reading beside the fix.

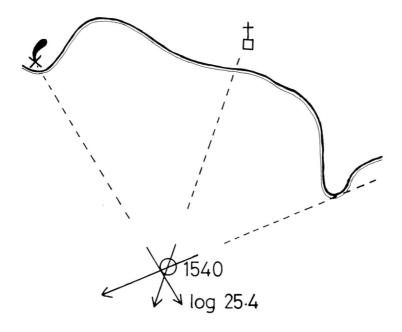

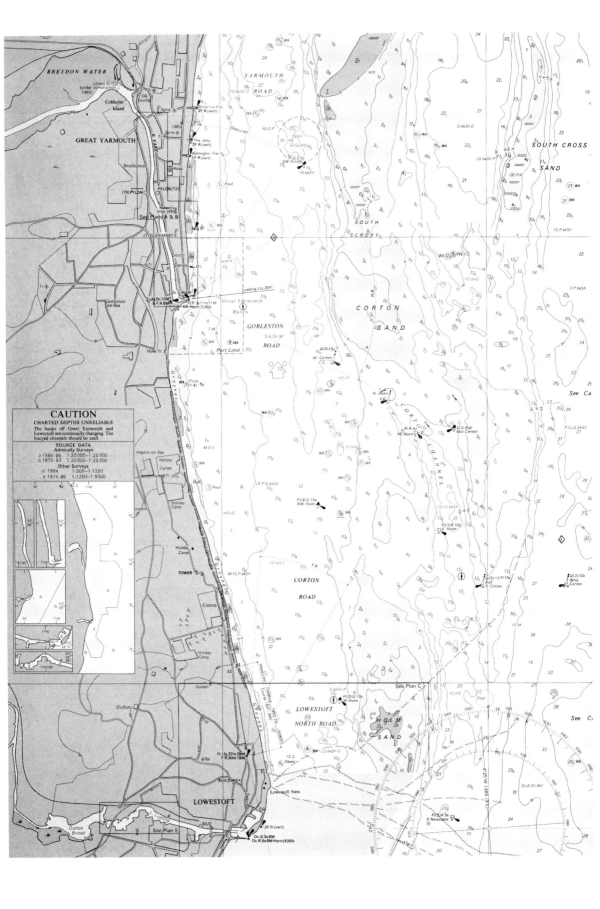

CAUTION
CHARTED DEPTHS UNRELIABLE
The banks off Great Yarmouth and
Lowestoft are continually changing. The
buoyed channels should be used.

SOURCE DATA
Admiralty Surveys
a 1984-86. 1:20 000-1:25 000
b 1979-83. 1:20 000-1:25 000
Other Surveys
c 1984 1:500-1:1250
d 1974-86 1:1250-1:5000

Figure 78 The blank dark area off Lowestoft indicates that that area is covered by a large scale plan elsewhere on the chart, which you can see in figure 74. When moving between charts and plans while navigating it is most important to check the scale, and ensure that distances are taken from the correct Latitude marks.

Figure 79 There are two concentric circular scales on this compass rose, the outer one giving True bearings and the inner one Magnetic. The angular difference between the two is called **Variation**, and it is noted in the centre of the rose, together with the amount by which it changes each year. On a recent chart this change should be negligible, and you can simply lay your parallel ruler on the centre and read off Magnetic courses and bearings direct

from the inner rose. A bearing from the hand-bearing compass can then be stepped across the chart until the rule aligns with the object from which it was taken, then a line of bearing drawn as in figure 77. If the Variation is more than about half a degree wrong, however, you must use the True rose, converting Magnetic bearings to True for plotting, and True courses to Magnetic for steering. The current Variation is calculated and applied to bearing or course according to the mnemonic C A D E T, which stands for Compass AdD East True. In short – to convert from Compass to True you add easterly Variation (or subtract westerly), and to go from True to Compass you reverse these. The same principle applies to changing between Compass and Magnetic courses when Deviation has to be applied (see figure 70): to go from Compass to Magnetic you add easterly Deviation.

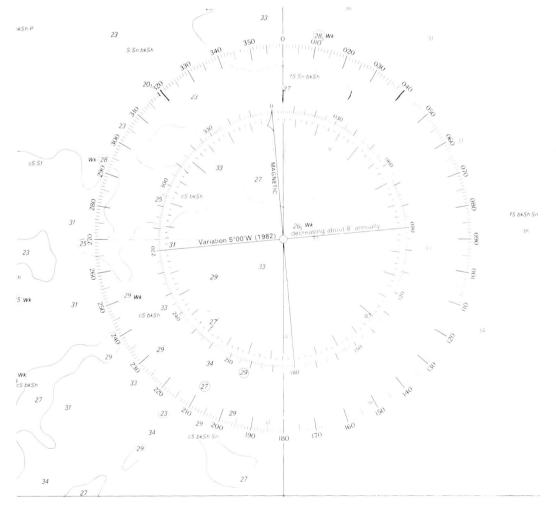

and also have details of your boat to give to the rescue services. Details of all these things will be found in Almanac and Pilot.

Once outside the harbour you should sail to a convenient point from which to set a direct course to the destination, or the first objective – in this case Lowestoft. At this point we should **fix** our position (see figure 77) and plot it on the chart, then draw a line on the chart from here to the destination. We then endeavour, in principle, to sail along this line, making due allowance for drift from leeway and tidal stream. This first fix is known as a **departure fix**, and can often be noted by eye. In this case it can simply be 'just off Yarmouth Harbour'; as on the chart in figure 78 you can see that we can safely plot a course direct from the end of the northern breakwater at Yarmouth to the starboard-hand buoy just to the north-west of Holm Sand (the drying bank off Lowestoft). If you then look at the larger scale chart of Approaches to Lowestoft in figure 74, you can see that from here it is barely a mile to the pair of cardinal buoys at the entrance to the inshore channel past Lowestoft. This is about half the range at which you will comfortably see buoys in fair weather.

Having drawn this line on the chart (lightly; so it can easily be rubbed out when finished with) we must find the direction to steer on the compass in order to follow it. We lay the parallel rulers alongside the line, then step them across the chart to the nearest **compass rose**, from which we can work out the course we must make good *over the ground* in order to get to the buoy. See figure 79. In figure 80 you can see how we then

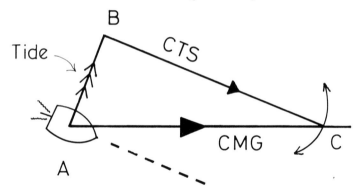

Figure 80 If the stream is setting as shown by the triple arrow (normal convention for plotting streams), and we want to make good a course over the ground as shown by CMG (Course Made Good), then it should be apparent that we must sail in the general direction of the pecked line to allow for the stream's effect. The precise course is calculated quite simply by first plotting a suitable vector A-B on the chart from our known position – usually the direction and distance the stream would carry us in one hour if we sat still. We then, in effect, need to sail for one hour from here (B), and end up on the CMG (in practice we would crab sideways along the CMG). Thus all we need do is set the compasses to the distance we estimate we will sail through the water in that one hour, centre them on B and mark where that distance crosses the CMG (C). The line B-C is then the Course To Steer (CTS) from A in order to move sideways along the CMG, and can be measured by stepping the parallel ruler across to the nearest compass rose. If we have already sailed a distance from A and want to find out where the stream has then set us to, we simply plot on the chart the course we have sailed, then mark on it the distance we have run (from the log). From this point we plot a vector of the total tidal set we have experienced during that time, and the end of that vector is where we are. If it is more than one hour, then a series of vectors will be needed, each plotted from the end of the previous one.

calculate the course we must actually steer *through the water* to allow for leeway and stream. As soon as we can see the buoy, however, we can steer for it by eye, making allowance for drift as explained in Chapter 4. It is extremely easy to allow wishful thinking to influence your identification of buoys etc, and it is vital that you check and double check all the details before assuming that it is the right one. A couple of miles to the north of the one we want (called the W Holm) is an identical green conical called the NW Holm, so care must be taken. Either plot a fix from shore objects, check the distance run on the log against the distance to the buoy (making allowance for stream) or simply sail close to the buoy and read the name on it! The NW Holm should be about half a mile to port as we pass it, although if we are steering to the east of the plotted track to allow for a stream setting southward, we will probably pass quite close to it. It will provide a handy check on progress.

Having navigated to the W Holm buoy on the chart in figure 77, we should change to the larger scale inset in figure 74 while we negotiate the wiggly bit past Lowestoft. At the top you can see the W Holm buoy, and you should be able to follow the succession of buoys marking the channel close by Lowestoft. There are two cardinals marking a shallow spot at the entrance; a port-hand can close to the coast; a west cardinal right outside the harbour entrance (not very clear as it is a correction drawn in); then the Pakefield green conical at the bottom of the chart, just west of the Newcombe Sand. You should be able to work out from what we have discussed so far where the channel is in relation to these buoys. Note the large open arrows showing the direction of the assumed flood stream (for buoyage purposes). If you look carefully at the depths, you can see that sailing along here is a simple matter of following the buoys, using the echo-sounder to confirm that we are in the deep water. Watch out for big fishing boats coming in and out of Lowestoft; the Pilot will advise on this and other matters.

At the Pakefield buoy we change back to the chart in figure 77 (the southern limit of which can be seen marked on the passage chart in figure 71) and continue past the S Newcombe green conical buoy to the east cardinal called E Barnard (just outside the darker shallow water, and in line with the lower edge of the inset chart of Southwold Harbour). We then go to the main passage chart in figure 71 and plot a course, as explained earlier, from this buoy to a convenient spot off Southwold Harbour (bottom left of figure 71). We can see from the inset plan of Southwold Harbour that the water is fairly shallow just outside so, as we should be arriving before half tide, we must aim to land up perhaps half a mile off, and take stock of the tidal situation then. When the tidal state is suitable (as we discussed earlier) we can enter the harbour, taking into account the comments and advice in the Pilot. A harbour as narrow and restricted as this should be entered under power by all but the most experienced of sailors. Have your anchor all ready to let go quickly in case of emergency – engine stopping, for example – and all warps and fenders prepared so that you can go straight alongside without fuss. Keep to the starboard side of the harbour in case others are coming out. If you have VHF, call the Harbour Master before entering to find out where to berth; otherwise berth at the nearest empty jetty then go and see him, or the local Yacht Club.

This knowledge should enable you safely to sail a simple coastal passage in fair weather, but further study of navigation ought to be made before undertaking anything more ambitious. See Chapter 15. Take enough food, clothing, fuel, etc to allow for twice the anticipated passage time, and plan to go only when the weather is likely to remain suitable for the return trip.

11
Emergency Routines

However competently you run your boat there may come a time when you find yourself in trouble. Some troubles are more serious than others but most, if handled calmly and capably, can be prevented from attaining the status of an emergency. Foresight is the key, and it is most important that you have a set of routines that you can immediately set in motion if a crisis develops. Clearly each situation will require individual handling, but the advantage of a predetermined routine is that you can immediately begin general constructive action before applying your mind to the particular aspects of that problem.

Grounding

This happens to the best of us, usually in our home ports through over-familiarity. The first rule is that if you intend chancing your arm on a short cut or an unknown harbour, then do so on the flood tide, never the ebb. If you run aground while the tide is rising it is a fairly simple matter to get off again. If you are quick and start her turning towards deep water the moment you feel her ground, then heel her over as far as possible to reduce the draft, you will very probably sail straight off. If not, then let go the anchor to stop you drifting into shallower water, and simply wait until she floats. If you are under power then go full astern immediately and try to motor off back the way you came. It can help to rock the boat from side to side (particularly with a long keel) if she is stuck in a soft bottom as this can free the grip on the keel. Moving the crew right forward in a long-keeled boat will also tend to lift the deepest part of the keel (aft), although this will not work with twin or fin keels as they are usually the same depth all along. Twin keels will also resist attempts to heel, as one keel will be forced down as the other lifts.

If you ground on a falling tide it is most unlikely that any of these measures will succeed, unless the tide is slack (very near High or Low Water at neaps), and the best thing to do is to immediately take a kedge anchor in the dinghy on a long warp and drop it as far away as possible in the deep water. Then heel her, weigh her down by the bow, and try to haul her off using winches if possible. But you must be quick. See photo 47. It is hard work dragging a long warp through the water by dinghy; much easier to flake all the warp in the dinghy then pay it out as you go. If that fails, you are stuck till the tide rises. On a smooth sandy bottom you can attempt to delude onlookers into thinking

Photo 47 Aground on a falling tide. The crew are heeling her over to reduce the draft, and the kedge has just been rowed out. They did get off.

the grounding was deliberate by going over the side and scrubbing the bottom (if the tide departs sufficiently)! On a rough, rocky bottom you must consider the possibility of damage or even holing and sinking. Explore the bottom with a boathook and try to get mattresses or something between the hull and any jagged protruberances that she may sit on. Bear in mind also that she may heel over a long way as the tide leaves her, so make sure all loose equipment above and below decks is secured.

If you ground on a steeply sloping bottom, then you must endeavour to make her lie up the slope rather than down it, by piling heavy weights (gas bottles,

anchor chain, dinghy filled with water etc) on the high side. If she lies down the slope she might fill with water before the tide lifts her. If there is a risk of this then secure all hatches as tightly as possible to prevent the water getting in.

Sinking

If you are taking in water through a hole in the hull there is a simple equation to consider: if it comes in faster than you can get it out again, you will, sooner or later, sink. Too many sailors have sublime faith in their bilge pumps to cope with this sort of thing, without ever sitting down with pencil and paper and working out the precise size of hole that all their pumps together could cope with. If they did, they would have a shock. The first priority in such a situation must always be to try and stem the inflow of water, to reduce it to

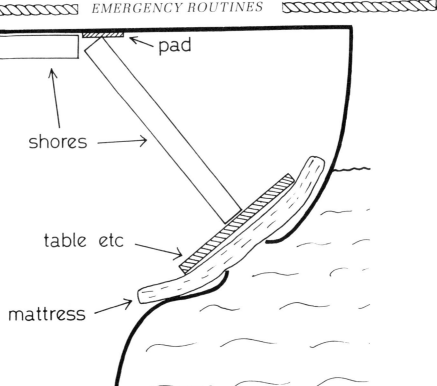

pad

shores →

table etc →

mattress →

Figure 81

proportions manageable by the pumps. If the hole is accessible from inside then jam a mattress over it and shore that up with a table and lengths of timber wedged against a bulkhead or whatever (see figure 81); or even get someone to sit on it: anything to slow down the flow of water into the boat. If the hole is not accessible from inside, then try to drag a sail or canvas sheet, with lines attached, across the hole on the outside. Haul it taut and lash it firmly.

Fire

The first thing to do is reduce the risk of the fire getting worse. Shut off fuel and gas at tank and bottle, in case pipes rupture. Shut all seacocks that have plastic hoses on them, if at all possible. The fire could

melt the hoses, and sinking the boat is a rather drastic way of putting out a fire. Alter course if you can so that the wind blows fire and smoke away from the main part of the boat and slow or stop to reduce the wind fanning the flames. Then attack the fire with suitable extinguishers: foam or dry powder are best for fuel fires (most likely), and water for simple bedding fires. Inert gas extinguishers often produce such toxic fumes in a small space that it is quite impossible to remain there. They are not advisable for boats. A fire should be approached like a wild animal: swing the extinguisher from side to side and steadily drive the fire into a corner where it can then be gradually smothered, working in from the front. If you simply squirt the extinguisher at the fire it will spray burning fuel everywhere. Cool all surrounding surfaces with water afterwards, and keep doing so until you are quite certain that no residual heat remains anywhere. Bear in mind that dry powder (most common type on small boats) smothers a fire but does not cool it; it remains hot underneath and can flare up again quite easily. Fire in a galley pan is best dealt with by carefully laying a fire blanket over it and leaving undisturbed until cool. The fire will go out due to lack of air.

Entering Fog

It is always best to stay safely in harbour when fog is forecast. Although there are electronic devices to help with both navigation and collision avoidance in fog (see Appendix 2), skill and experience are needed to use them properly. Besides which there is no pleasure in the dangerous and nerve-wracking business of sailing about in fog. If you do get caught out, however, there are some basic precautions that should be rigidly adhered to:

1 Fix your position as soon as you see fog coming, before all land and sea marks are obscured. Then keep very careful track of your progress by dead reckoning (see Chapter 10).

2 Post lookouts (one for'ard) to both look, and listen for foghorns and engines. Sound your own horn at the required intervals (see Appendix 4). Listen down below with an ear against the hull: engine noise travels much further in water than in air.

3 Warm up the engine so that it is ready for immediate use, then shut it off to reduce noise as much as possible while listening. Only use the engine if you cannot sail fast enough for good steerage.

4 If in a **shipping lane** where commercial shipping congregates (see Almanac), then get out as fast as possible, using engine if necessary. Head inshore for shallow water where the big ships cannot go; and where you may be able to anchor until the fog lifts.

5 In very busy waters – shipping lane junctions, approaches to large commercial harbours and so on – have the crew don lifejackets and remain on deck. If you are in collision with a big ship, the boat could sink in seconds. If you have a partially deflated inflatable dinghy on deck, then blow it up and prepare it for immediate use.

6 If you hear a foghorn, try to have all the crew estimate its bearing, then average out the results; it is very difficult to accurately determine the direction of sound in fog. Then keep checking the bearing to see if it is changing or remains steady (see Chapter 4). Sound your own foghorn immediately after hearing another.

7 If you are in radiation fog (see Chapter 8) then send a man up the mast in case it is very low-lying. He may be able to see high land or the masts of other boats over the top of it.

8 If a ship suddenly appears out of the fog very close and heading for you, the risk of actual collision can be reduced by rapidly altering course directly towards her bow if it is for'ard of your beam, or directly away from it if it is abaft your beam. You then present the smallest possible target, and there is a good chance that her bowwave will push you clear of her stem. This really is a last resort if there is clearly no hope of motoring flat out to get clear.

It can be very difficult, especially at night, to predict the onset of fog. It is, however, usually preceded by a feeling of clammy coldness and dampness. Moisture will begin to form on the boat like dew as the fog starts to condense out of the air. Navigation lights will look hazy. In daylight the visibility can be assessed by throwing something over the side (ball of paper etc) and watching it out of sight.

Man Overboard

It is important to realise just how difficult it can be even to find a man in the water, never mind get him back on board. At

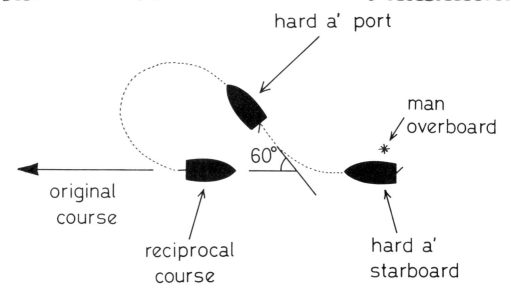

Figure 82 Continue the initial swing until you have gone about 60° from the original course then put on full opposite helm. Continue like that until you have come right round to the reciprocal of the original course, and that should take you back to him. Practice will enable you to assess the best angle for your boat, and also the distance the man will be ahead of you when you reach the reciprocal course.

night it is well-nigh impossible unless he has a light (on lifejacket or thrown lifebelt); and in rough weather not even this will help you find him. Many boats carry a dhan buoy (with a tall pole and flag) attached to the lifebelts and the increased visibility of this considerably improves the chances of finding a man in rough weather (assuming it is thrown over quickly enough). Thus prevention is all-important. Harnesses should be worn at all times in rough weather and at night, and whenever one crew is alone on watch, even sat in the cockpit. The safety line should be attached to a strongpoint (not guardrail), and adjusted in length so that the man cannot actually go over the side.

If the worst does happen there are a number of actions that should be taken instantly (ideally all together):

1 Throw lifebelt to man (with light at night)
2 Call out 'Man overboard' to alert rest of crew
3 Watch the man constantly; and never take your eyes off him
4 Under power – swing stern and propeller hard away from man
5 Under sail – swing immediately onto a beam reach
6 Press Decca 'Man Overboard Marker' if fitted (for position)

You now have protected him from the propeller (if motoring); kept him afloat and more visible; have him in sight; and made the first manoeuvre towards re-covering him. The initial alert is over and you can (and should) set about calmly to return and pick him up. A modern small yacht under power will probably turn sharply and quickly enough for you to simply continue turning hard round until you get back to him. Approach slightly to weather of the man and pick him up on the lee side of the boat, where the sea will be calmer and the freeboard low. Stop the engine completely just before reaching him, to avoid the risk of a turning propeller. A larger or less manoeuvrable craft should, after the initial swing, execute a **Williamson Turn** as shown in figure 82.

If you are sailing you should continue the beam reach for about ten boat lengths then go about, right round onto a beam reach on the other tack. This course should then take you more or less right back to the man. Make the final approach on a close reach, trimming sails as required to adjust speed so that you stop with him amidships to leeward, the easiest place at which to recover him as it is low and subject to less motion than bow or stern.

Actually getting a wet, cold, perhaps even unconscious man aboard can be quite a task. A good, simple and effective method is that taught for entering liferafts: bounce the man up and down a few times in the water to gain momentum then give a mighty extra heave as he comes up. Once part of him is on deck the rest will be a lot easier to drag over. It should be possible to unfasten the ends of the guardrails so they can be flattened onto the deck to give a clear deck edge over which to drag him. If he is conscious then a boarding ladder will be a great help. Other methods worth considering are securing a halyard round below his shoulders with a bowline and hauling to take a lot of the weight; or slipping a sail beneath him in the water, secured to the rail fore and aft and lifting him with a halyard on the outer third corner. He could even be scooped straight into this as you approach him.

Dismasting

The first thing you do *not* do if the mast falls over the side is start the engine. There will be so much rope and wire and suchlike floating about that you will almost certainly wrap something round the prop. The initial action must be to get mast and all rigging back on board and lashed down securely before starting the engine. It is difficult to give detailed advice on the best way of doing this, as

the situation is likely to be somewhat shambolic. You will, however, find it much easier to get the mast back onboard if you disconnect as much of the rigging as possible from the boat and let it float clear, so that it does not hinder the movement of the mast. The boat will swing downwind of all the gear so everything should stream away to windward and hopefully become less tangled. Make sure something holds the mast to the boat during all this or you may suddenly find the whole lot disappearing over the horizon.

If you cannot get the mast on deck then try to lash it alongside so that all rigging is clear of the propeller. This may entail the risk of serious damage if the weather is rough and you must be prepared to simply cut the whole lot adrift if necessary. If you do this, then inform the nearest coast radio station of its whereabouts using a SAYCURITAY call: it could be a danger to other boats. See Appendix 4. The alternative is to let it all stream from the bow, whereupon the boat should lie quite comfortably head to wind, and wait for the seas to calm sufficiently for you to try getting it all on deck again. When everything is sorted out you can either motor to the nearest harbour to get it reassembled, or rig up some sort of jury mast using the boom or spinnaker pole.

Steering Failure

If the failure is in the deck gear – broken tiller or wheel linkage – then you have only to dig out and fit the emergency tiller. Make sure, before you need it, that this both fits and works (without jamming on the cockpit coaming for example). If it is steel (as they often are), then you should have the compass swung with it stowed, and also with it in use, as the Deviation may be different. Two separate Deviation cards might be necessary. See Chapter 10.

If the failure is in the rudder you will have to rig up some sort of jury system, which can be difficult if the rudder is not hung on the outside of a transom stern. If the boat has a long keel and a well balanced rig, you may find it fairly easy to steer with the sails. Back the jib no more than absolutely necessary, then steer by adjusting the trim of the mainsail or the backing of the jib. If you cannot do this then you will have to devise some sort of rudder or steering oar to lash onto the stern, using perhaps a spinnaker boom and a door or cockpit grating. Lashed to the backstay, this might do the trick in reasonable weather.

Fouled Propeller or Rudder

It is all too easy to get a trailing rope caught round the propeller when motoring, especially while manoeuvring amongst mooring lines, and great care should be taken to keep ropes away from the stern at such times. It is also possible to pick up lines from fishing floats out at sea, especially at night, either round the prop or round the rudder if it is hung clear of the after end of the keel. If the rudder is on a skeg then it is a good idea to fix a wire from the skeg to the keel, to make ropes slide clear under the rudder. It is also possible to fit special rope cutters to propshafts that will automatically cut away any rope that tangles in the prop.

Failing these gadgets you could find yourself in bother. A rope round the rudder can often be pushed down clear by using a long pole with a rowlock or something lashed to the end, or possibly by lowering a length of chain onto it with a long line. If it jams between the hull and the top of the rudder, however, you will probably have to cut it on one side and haul it clear from the other.

A rope round the prop is more of a problem. If the engine does not stop anyway, then stop it and disable it to ensure that it cannot fire up as you try to pull the rope clear. Remove the plug leads from a petrol engine, or decompress the cylinders in a diesel. Then try hauling on one end of the rope and turn the propshaft

by hand at the same time. With a bit of juggling you may be able to free it by turning in the opposite direction to the way it was turning when it fouled.

Usually, however, no amount of pulling and turning will shift it. Artificial fibres tend to wrap round the shaft then melt into a solid mass due to the friction. The only solution is to cut it off with a hacksaw or serrated blade; smooth blades are quite ineffectual, however sharp. This generally entails hanging over the side of the dinghy with the blade lashed to a boathook or something, and great care must be taken to hold the dinghy securely so that it does not move as the blade is sawn back and forth. A second man should sit in the dinghy and hold onto the one doing the cutting.

Rescue Procedure

If you should ever get into serious trouble at sea and need rescuing, there are a few things you should bear in mind. All seamen are obliged to give assistance to others in distress (and that includes you if you find someone else in trouble), but that assistance extends only to saving human lives, not property (eg boats). If anyone does rescue a vessel they are entitled to claim salvage, and that includes lifeboats (although they rarely do). The amount payable is a proportion of the value of the boat, depending basically on the difficulty of the task, and it can be a considerable sum. If you simply require a tow into harbour then agree a fixed fee for the job with the rescue skipper beforehand, in front of witnesses on both boats.

If you are rescued by a commercial vessel, then the more control you take of the operation the smaller will be the eventual salvage claim. If possible, supply the tow rope and any equipment, and instruct the rescue skipper as to precisely what you want doing. For an inexperienced yachtsman in real trouble, however, this is a counsel of perfection that might well cause more trouble than it is designed to prevent. If a lifeboat is involved, then do exactly as the coxswain tells you.

If a rescue involves a helicopter or a big ship, then certain precautions must be taken. If you are jumping from a small yacht onto a rope ladder down a ship's side, then do so when the yacht is on top of a wave so that she drops away from you instead of rising and crushing you before you can get up the ladder. Being towed by a big ship can produce all sorts of problems, mainly because the slowest speed at which they can go while maintaining steering control is likely to be too fast for towing a small yacht. There is a real risk of a yacht being dragged under. Towlines should be secured to the strongest possible place – round the mast, for example – as the normal fittings on a yacht are unlikely to take the terrific strains involved. They must, however, be led from the stem somehow, so that she is towed from the bow.

A helicopter produces a very strong downdraught of air from its rotors, so all loose gear that might get blown about or sucked into its engines must be secured before it arrives. The wire that it lowers for rescuing people is vulnerable to catching on things. If it does, the helicopter could be dragged out of control, so *never* attach it to anything, even for a moment. Masts and rigging are a danger to the wire and helicopter rescues are best made from a liferaft or dinghy trailed a long way astern of the boat.

Finally, you would be surprised how many people never bother to write a letter of thanks to the local lifeboat Secretary or the Commanding Officer of the helicopter's base. It seems a small enough, but thoughtful thing to do. A donation to the RNLI would not seem out of place either, especially if your valuable boat has been rescued.

12

The Auxiliary Engine

Although it is most satisfying for a sailor to handle his boat under sail, there are two very good reasons for having an auxiliary engine. The first is to get busy people back onto their moorings in time to go to work the next day, and the second is the fact that harbours and rivers are so crowded these days that it is, in truth, unseamanlike to not have the manoeuvrability of an engine standing by to get you out of trouble.

The best type of auxiliary, in my view, is a small inboard diesel engine; which is economical, reliable, sheltered from the rain and the sea, and uses fuel that is far safer from fire and explosion than is petrol. An inboard installation can also run a generator to charge batteries for lighting and electronics, and a powered bilge pump. See photo 48. A very small boat, however, may simply not have the space and will have to settle for an outboard; preferably permanently installed so that it is immediately available when required. See photo 49. Whichever you have, you must resist the temptation of the sailor to forget its existence when it is not in use. A boat is a harsh environment for an engine, and if you want yours to work when you need it, you must look after it.

Essential running maintenance for a small engine is neither difficult nor time consuming, and I recommend the following routine before each trip (whether you intend using the engine or not):

1 – Check oil levels in engine and gearboxes
2 – Check level of fresh water in header tank if water cooled
3 – Check fuel level in tank
4 – Check electrolyte levels in batteries
5 – Check tension and condition of drive belts (alternator etc)
6 – Check security of pipe clips and condition of hoses
7 – Check seacock filter clear and seacock free to open
8 – Screw down stern-tube greaser and grease cups (pumps etc)
9 – Check condition of wiring and that all connections are tight

With practice all this will take less than ten minutes and will, in conjunction with

opposite
Photo 48 A typical small inboard auxiliary. This one is petrol and fits under the steps into the cabin. Note sterntube greaser top right, and belt-driven generator to charge batteries.

Photo 49 A neat way of stowing an outboard so that it is ready for instant use.

the maintenance in Chapter 13 and the engine handbook, go a long way towards ensuring trouble-free motoring. You should then start the engine and leave it running in neutral while leaving your berth – partly so that it is instantly available in emergency, and partly to charge the batteries. Check that cooling water is coming out, that oil pressure is correct, and that the alternator is charging. Check also that both ahead and astern gears work.

For troubleshooting if the engine goes wrong, I strongly advise you to get a book on your type of engine (see Appendix 3), in which you should find details of likely problems and how to solve them, as well as general information on the workings of the engine and ancillaries. The better you understand the operation of your engine, the more easily will you be able to cure breakdowns. See also Appendix 4.

Handling Characteristics

Competent handling of a boat under power depends not only on practice but also on an understanding of the propeller's behaviour in the water, and the effect that the hull shape will have on this. In simple terms we can say that a propeller is much like a screw that winds through the water pulling the boat after it. At the same time, however, the twist in the blades makes it act something like a paddlewheel set sideways across the stern, and it will paddle the stern to one side as it goes forward. This is known as **paddlewheel effect** and it is at its strongest when the propeller is trying hardest to move the boat; eg from rest (particularly when going astern), and when reversing the direction of the engine. The direction in which it pulls depends on the direction of rotation of the propeller, some being **right-handed** and some **left-handed**. What happens should be clear from figure 83. As the boat gets under way and the effort to push it diminishes, so does the effect. Paddlewheel effect is greatest with a large,

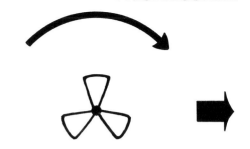

Right-handed prop ahead

Left-handed prop astern

Figure 83

slow-revving propeller, and very slight with small, fast-revving props such as on outboards.

The effectiveness of the rudder for steering depends entirely on the speed of the water passing it. This can be utilised when under power, as a burst ahead on the engine will wash a rapid flow of water across the rudder, thus making her turn very much more rapidly than she will from just her speed through the water. If your propeller is abaft the rudder (occasionally found on sailing boats), this effect will not be available to you. Swivelling outboards do not need this assistance as they push water away from the stern in the direction they are pointing, so steer very effectively when in gear. When out of gear they will not steer at all.

When turning under power the boat will pivot around a point roughly one third of her length from the bow, thus causing the stern to swing out wide of the turn – an important point to consider in tight situations. A boat with a short fin keel will turn more quickly than one with a long keel, there being less underwater hull forward resisting the turn. This will also make paddlewheel effect more noticeable on a short-keel boat, especially when going astern. The wind can have a marked effect on the handling of a sailing boat under power, due to the windage of spars and rigging. Generally this windage is greatest forward, so tending to make the bow blow off, sometimes quite strongly. A side effect of this is that when going astern, the bow blowing off rapidly will cause the stern to swing quite sharply up towards the wind. When going astern you must also understand that the pivot point around which the boat swings when turning moves aft to a position about one third of her length from the stern, so making the bow swing out wide of the turn. A very useful technique for turning sharply under power is to give a succession of short bursts ahead to throw the wash of the prop across the angled rudder. This will turn her much more rapidly and in a shorter length (as the boat swings but does not have time to gather way) than will simply putting the rudder over and going slow ahead. It is particularly useful for driving the bow round into the wind. The precise effects of all these factors on your boat in varying conditions can only be found from experience, so get out into a wide open space and practise.

Handling a Boat Under Power

Although this is generally easier than handling under sail (mainly because you can put the engine in reverse gear to stop!), it should be apparent from the last section that there is rather more to it than driving a car. Anchoring and picking up a mooring under power are fairly straight-forward as it is relatively easy to judge the right moment to go astern and stop. Bear in mind, however, that on going astern the paddlewheel effect is likely to swing the bow away from a buoy, so aim slightly to the other side such that she will then swing towards the buoy as you stop. Anchor cable can be laid out straighter and more quickly by going slow astern after letting go, but remember again paddlewheel effect and the windage of the bow. When all the cable has been veered you should go astern again to dig in the

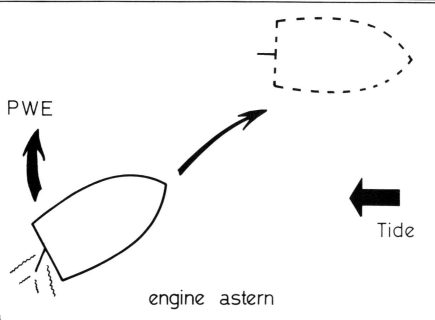

Figure 84

anchor and check that it is not dragging. Berthing alongside a jetty, however, requires more thought.

In figure 84 we have a boat coming alongside port side to, with a right-handed propeller. The approach should be made at about 30° to the line of the jetty, then the tiller put over to swing her alongside as you get close. At the same time go astern to stop, and the paddle-wheel effect of the prop will pull your stern across towards the jetty. If you judge it correctly the boat will stop alongside the jetty, lying parallel to it. With a left-handed prop the paddlewheel effect will be reversed, and this approach should be used for berthing starboard side to.

A slightly different technique is required when berthing in such a way that paddlewheel effect on going astern will swing the stern out instead of in. In this situation the approach should be made more slowly and at a steeper angle to the jetty, then a burst of forward power given as the tiller goes over, in order to start the stern swinging rapidly in. The paddle-wheel effect on going astern to stop will

Figure 85 The white arrows show how bow and stern will swing around the white pivot when going ahead with the outboard at the angle indicated. The black arrows and black pivot show the behaviour on going astern.

then counteract and slow this inward swing of the stern. Once again, if judged correctly these forces will combine to stop you alongside and parallel with the jetty.

Outboard engines require a technique of their own. Paddlewheel effect is negligible, and the stern is swung in towards the quay by turning the outboard on going astern so that it pulls the stern across in the desired direction. See figure 85. It is most important to realise that outboard motors will not steer in neutral, as there is no water being thrust out of them by the prop. Use the boat's rudder.

Getting away from a berth is much easier under power than it is under sail as you can utilise the technique of 'springing'. This, quite simply, consists of slipping all mooring warps except the fore-spring, then motoring slowly ahead against this with the helm over to swing the stern out. A good fender will be required right forward. The spring will stop you going ahead, and the stern will swing out well clear so that you can slip the spring and go astern into open water before turning. See figure 86. You can do the same thing by going astern against a backspring to swing the bow out but it is not so effective, and you run the risk of clobbering the propeller (especially an outboard) on any obstructions protruding from the jetty underwater.

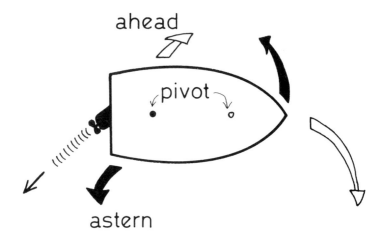

ahead

pivot

astern

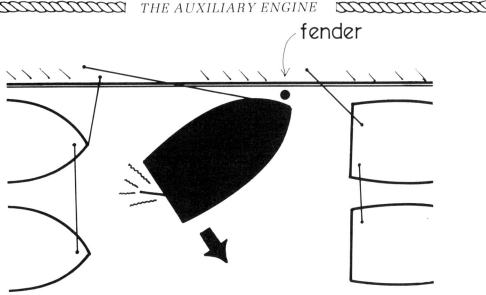

Figure 86 It is most important that the spring is led from right for'ard or the boat will not swing out properly, as the bow will swing in and jam against the wall. The amount of swing required will depend on your paddlewheel effect and the wind influence when you go astern to clear the berth. Visualise what will happen when you do so, before you slip!

The Effects of Wind and Tide

As with anchoring, mooring and berthing under sail, the approach to a jetty should always be made into the tide, unless the tide is negligible and there is a strong wind. If the wind is in the same direction as the tide then it will simply help to slow you down, although during the approach it will actually blow on the outside of the bow and you may need to give the odd burst of power with the tiller over in order to stop her head swinging into the jetty. If the wind is from astern you must guard against coming in too fast, but on going astern the stern of the boat will tend to 'seek the wind' so this will help to hold you straight. If the wind is blowing onto the jetty you should aim to berth a couple of feet clear so that the wind can blow you down alongside. If the wind is off the jetty you must approach steeply and give a

good burst of power with tiller over (as for opposing paddlewheel effect), then get a headrope ashore as quickly as possible before the bow blows away, as it will the moment you go astern.

Turning in a Small Space

Most modern sailing cruisers with short keels will turn very quickly, especially if the technique of short bursts ahead is used. If a three point turn has to be made, however, it should always be made first in such a direction that on going astern paddlewheel effect will pull her round the desired way. With a right-handed prop the initial turn should be to starboard. The moment she begins to swing (before gathering way ahead), go hard astern and the paddlewheel effect will continue the swing tightly round until you are pointing back the way you came. With a left-handed prop you should make the initial turn to port. Ideally, the initial turn should also be made away from the wind so that the stern seeking it will help further to pull her round as you go astern. An outboard will turn sharply round either way, by swinging it round on going astern so that it pulls the stern in the desired direction.

Motor-Sailing

This is a useful trick, consisting of motoring and sailing at the same time, and is particularly helpful when bashing to windward in a rough sea. By running the engine at fairly slow revs as you sail you will find that the boat sails much faster and points closer to the wind. You will need to experiment with the revs to find the most efficient combination but in principle you need far less revs than would be required for such a speed under engine alone. This is a much more efficient and comfortable way of getting to windward than simply motoring straight into wind and sea. It is important, once the speed of the engine is set up, to in effect ignore the engine and sail the boat as if it was not running. Any attempt to pinch too close to the wind will be extremely detrimental to both performance and comfort. The converse of this is that you will be much more comfortable with some sail set when motoring in calms and light breezes, as the sails will reduce considerably the tendency to roll, especially in a beam sea.

Towing

This is something you may be called upon to do from time to time when you are under power, if you find someone in a bit of bother. A simple tow in calm water – pulling someone off the mud perhaps – involves little more than attaching a strong rope between strong fittings on the two boats then very gradually taking the weight until the towed boat begins to move. Try not to jerk the rope or you may part it, or pull out of the deck the fitting it is attached to. The towed boat should steer so as to keep the towrope taut all the time. If there is any wind or tidal stream you will have to plan carefully to avoid drifting into danger. Keep the towrope well clear of your rudder and propeller. If the boat is drifting in open water then approach and cross his bow from leeward, passing the towrope as you go. Get under way as quickly as possible in case you drift into an awkward position.

If you need to tow a boat in or out of a berth or a tight spot, it will be best to tow him alongside. Secure to him as you would a jetty, but keep all warps as tight

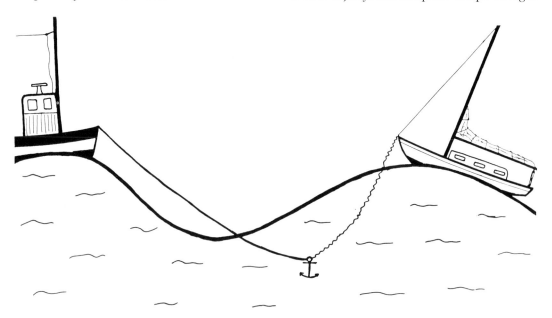

Figure 87

as possible and position yourself so that your propeller is abaft his stern, as this will improve your power and manoeuvrability. When you turn, the drag of the boat alongside will cause you to turn more tightly towards him than away. It will also reduce both your acceleration and stopping power.

Towing at sea, because of the constant yanking of waves, requires a different technique. Some means of cushioning the shocks must be used. The simplest is to attach the towrope to his anchor, then have him veer sufficient cable so that the whole towline hangs down quite deeply in the water. See figure 87. Build up speed very slowly and maintain a towing speed that keeps the towline in the water so that it can absorb shocks by springing up and down. Adjust the length so that both boats rise to a wave at the same time. Protect the towrope against chafe in fairleads etc, and have an axe or sharp knife handy to cut the tow in emergency. Secure the towline so that it can be easily cast off under strain (see Chapter 6).

13
Essential Maintenance

Maintenance, even for a fibreglass boat, is a big and often complex subject, many things requiring experienced professional attention. In Appendix 3 you will find recommended books on the subject, but here let us look at the simple general running maintenance that will prevent the condition of the boat deteriorating.

Sails and Rigging

There are two main problem areas with modern synthetic sails: the stitching stands proud of the cloth and is thus prone to chafe; and the cloth slowly deteriorates in strong sunlight, coloured sails fading quite rapidly. All head sails should be stowed below in bags when not in use, and a cover should fit over the mainsail on the boom. Regular checks should be made of the stitching, and any worn areas resewn immediately or the slight weakness might cause a strong wind to tear out a whole seam of stitching. All the sails should be sent to a sailmaker for inspection when you lay up for winter.

Standing rigging is normally made of stainless steel wire these days, and requires no maintenance. Unlike galvanised wire, however, stainless will work-harden in time and become prone to failure from fatigue. Broken strands will indicate this, and the rigging must be renewed. Wire running rigging is much more flexible and does not suffer in the same way, giving many years of reliable service. All wire should, however, be checked at least annually for broken strands (usually where the wire enters end fittings or at the crowns of eyes), and replaced if any are found.

Ropes – halyards, sheets, mooring warps – should be checked regularly for the slightest sign of chafe, and the cause of any tracked down and attended to before the rope chafes enough to be weakened. Renew any frayed whippings before the end of the rope starts to fall apart. Sheets often chafe against shrouds and spreaders and in worn fairleads, and halyards chafe on worn sheaves in the mast. Plastic piping slit and fitted round the lower parts of shrouds will reduce chafe on sheets, and the leads of halyards and sheets should be checked to ensure that they do not chafe unnecessarily. Cover spreader ends with proprietary plastic fittings, tennis balls or masses of waterproof tape. Replace any sheaves etc causing chafe to halyards or sheets. All rope and rigging should be washed in fresh water then thoroughly dried and inspected before storing for the winter. Cut out damaged sections of ropes and re-use the remainder by splicing together, or use as two short lengths.

All screw shackles should be lightly greased, and those fitted permanently must be moused with wire (see Chapter 6). Bent or stiff shackles should be replaced: they could prove a danger if they jam in an urgent situation. The bearing surfaces of shackles and pins holding standing rigging etc should be checked for wear at least annually, and replaced if more than very slightly worn. Bottle-screws should be lightly greased, then locked with wire or split pins to prevent unscrewing as locking nuts are not reliable. Replace immediately any that are cracked or bent. The forestay bottlescrew must be free to bend in all directions to allow for the jib flapping, so must be secured to the stemhead fitting with a flexible toggle or two shackles.

Hull

The basic principle of hull maintenance – steel, wood or fibreglass – is to keep the water out. Steel will rust in the presence of air and water; wood will rot in the presence of fresh water (but not in sea-water, so regular deck scrubbing with the latter is to be recommended); and fibreglass can absorb water through the **gelcoat** (which is not waterproof), becoming gradually saturated and heavier, and prone to a form of blistering known as **osmosis**. Foam sandwich boats can literally fall apart if saturated with sufficient water. Wood and steel boats should be regularly touched up with paint whenever damage or peeling is discovered. Peeling and 'bubbled' paintwork not only allows the weather to get at the bare hull, but also holds water permanently against it, so speeding up considerably the rot or corrosion. All loose paint should be scraped away from the faulty area which must be thoroughly dried and sand-papered before paint is applied. Treat rusty steel with a wire brush then a derusting agent before painting.

Fibreglass gelcoat can be scratched by dirt, so wash frequently with fresh water and washing up liquid. Once a year or so, clean thoroughly with a proprietary cleaner (non abrasive) and apply wax polish to both waterproof and protect from scratching by dirt and dust. Do not use a silicone polish as this will be impossible to remove should you ever decide to paint the hull. Gelcoat can be permanently waterproofed by a coating of special epoxy paint, but this is an expensive process best done professionally, as temperature and humidity are critical for successful results. If your type of boat has a history of osmosis troubles (some types seem more prone than others), or you keep her in conditions likely to produce it (long periods in warm fresh water are worst), then it might be a good idea to have the bottom so treated. Old scruffy boats can be made as new by epoxy painting the topsides. Damage to gelcoat should be repaired immediately (to stop water getting in) with a proprietary gel-coat repair kit of a suitable colour. Dry the damaged area thoroughly, then follow the instructions on the kit.

Damage inside the boat should also be repaired or painted promptly. Fresh water sitting in corners inside a wood or steel boat will cause rot or corrosion in no time, while fibreglass boats will absorb water and cause rot in timber strengthening that may be embedded in the fibreglass (engine beds and so on).

Under the waterline your boat, unless she spends most of her life out of the water, should be painted with **anti-fouling paint**, which will discourage weed, barnacles and sundry marine life from setting up home on it, to the great detriment of your speed. Fouling varies from area to area, both in type and degree (usually very little in fresh water), so use the anti-fouling paint most commonly employed in your home port. Take advice from the chandler or boatyard as some types cannot be painted over other types. Specialist advice is needed for anti-fouling steel or aluminium hulls as the metal in the paint can react with the hull (see later section on Electrolysis). Anti-fouling will also help prevent marine worms from eating a wooden boat. It should not be applied over echo-sounder transducers or **anodes** (below) or they will not work.

Engine and Electrics

Besides the simple running maintenance discussed in Chapter 12 you should religiously carry out at the specified intervals all maintenance listed in the engine handbook. The best way to maintain any machinery in good order – mechanical or electrical – is to use it regularly. This prevents internal corrosion which is so often the cause of unreliability. Keep electrics and electronics dry. Keep diesel fuel tanks as full as possible to prevent condensation depositing water in the fuel. Drain water and muck from the tank's sludge trap frequently to prevent rough weather (or even high pressure filling) from swirling it up into the fuel system.

If you drop an outboard into the water then hose it down with fresh water as soon as possible. Remove sparkplugs and dry them. Drain off any water in the fuel tank, and drain the oil from the gearbox, replacing it if it is watery. Turn the engine over a number of times to remove water from cylinders; leave to dry for a while, then squirt a little oil in the cylinders and get it running again as soon as possible.

Electrolysis

This is a form of electrical corrosion that occurs when two different metals are immersed close together in seawater. Electricity flows from one metal to the other through the seawater, in the process of which the first metal gradually disintegrates. It can even happen with a single metal, due to slight impurities in the surface. It is much aggravated by any free electricity flowing about the boat – from poorly earthed electrical and electronic

equipment – and is worse in steel and wooden boats than in fibreglass ones, due to the greater amount of metal in the construction. Propshafts, propellers and seacocks can suffer from it in fibreglass boats and in wooden ones it can weaken the fastenings holding the planks to the hull.

Figure 88 gives a list of metals, and if any two of these are immersed in seawater the one higher up the list will corrode. The further apart they are in the list, the faster will be the corrosion, so if metals do have to be mixed underwater they should be as close as possible in the table. Bronze propellers should always be on passive stainless steel shafts, not the active type. Note the position of graphite; do not use graphite grease underwater or your seacocks might fall out! Note also the position of zinc. This will corrode in preference to any other metal and lumps of it, known as **sacrificial anodes**, are fastened to the boat close to metal fittings underwater, thus ensuring that any electrolytic action will corrode the anode in preference to the fitting. See photo 50. They should also be fastened directly onto metal rudders and outboard motor legs.

Electro-chemical Series of Metals
Zinc
Aluminium
Steel
Iron
Stainless Steel (Active type)
Lead
Brass
Copper
Bronze
Stainless Steel (Passive type)
Graphite
Gold

Figure 88

Photo 50

Renew them when two thirds eaten. Specialist advice should be taken for the electrolytic protection of steel, aluminium and ferro-cement boats.

Much can be done to reduce this corrosion by ensuring that all electrical equipment is properly earthed. Professional advice should be taken, but in principle a thick earth strap should bond all items together such that leakage of current to earth does not pass *through* any equipment, but merely touches it en route. Whole engines can corrode if current is passed through them with all that hot seawater swirling about. Make sure seacocks are bonded to the engine if they are connected to plastic pipes or batteries will be set up between seacock and engine, seawater conducting electricity through the pipe and causing the seacock to decay. Always turn battery isolating switches off when they are not in use, to prevent stray currents leaking to earth.

These switches should be double pole (disconnecting both wires).

Winter Maintenance

The following list of jobs should be attended to each year when you lay up for winter:

Engine: clean and winterise if laying up (see manual); engineer to test condition of engine and list work needed

Cooling system: clean sludge out of pipes, fittings and thermostat; test thermostat in hot water

Lubricating system: change oil in engine and gearboxes while hot from running; renew all filters

Fuel system: drain and clean tank (close cock to keep diesel in pipes); clean or renew all filters; clean carburetter float chamber; blow through jets; send diesel injectors for service

Electrical system: take battery, starter and generator ashore if laying up; keep battery charged and have it heavy discharge tested; check brushes and commutator in starter and generator; remove batteries from torches etc to prevent leakage; move electronic equipment to warm, dry place ashore or use regularly to keep dry

Ignition system: renew sparkplugs, points (inc. magneto) and condenser; check all HT and LT connections for tightness and cleanliness

Control systems: inspect, refurbish and grease steering gear; oil or grease all linkages (throttle etc)

Drive system: check plummer block, propshaft flange and stern gland (repack if it has been leaking); check security and condition of propeller (file smooth small nicks; send away for larger damage); spray propeller with lacquer

Water system: drain, clean and sterilise tank; leave tank and all piping empty if frost expected

Heads: drain and clean; repack pump glands; leave bowl and pipes empty if frost expected

Seacocks: strip, clean and lightly grease; bed in with grinding paste if leaking; leave closed

Outboard engine: flush through with fresh water

Pumps: strip and check impellers (cooling water and bilge); renew gaskets; strip and check diaphragm and valves (hand bilge pumps)

Anodes: check, and renew if two thirds gone

Windlass: clean and lubricate; cover from weather

Cockpit: cover to keep rain water out

Liferaft: keep ashore; send for service every two years

Fire extinguishers: keep onboard in case of fire; have serviced every two years or when marked

Compass: keep ashore clear of all metal and magnets; have professionally swung on refitting or after major work on boat

Dinghy: wash with fresh water; inspect and repair; store ashore upside down and well supported; dry inflatable and send away for all but minor repairs

Hull of boat: wash with fresh water; repair and repaint

Bilges: clean with Bilgex or similar; leave open for ventilation

Lockers: clean out and leave open to ventilate

Chain: spread out and inspect; renew markings

Ropes: wash with fresh water; dry, inspect and hang in well ventilated space

Sails: wash with fresh water and dry; inspect and send to sailmaker for all but minor repairs

Fastenings: check security of all deck fittings, rudder hangings, A-brackets etc

Buoyancy aids: remove ashore; inspect; store in dry place

Bedding, food etc: remove and store in dry place ashore

Trailer: wash with fresh water; repair and paint as necessary; repack grease in wheel hubs

Charts & books: correct up to date (self or chart agent)

14

Buying a Sailing Cruiser

It is better to postpone a decision about buying a boat until you have some experience sailing other people's. This will help immeasurably in the difficult task of deciding, from the huge variety available, just what sort of boat you really want, as will the opportunity to talk with seasoned sailors. This can be done easily if you have sailing friends, but if not then I would strongly recommend a week or so at an RYA-recognised sailing school. Not only will you have some experience actually sailing and seeing different types of sailing cruisers, but you will also meet and talk with other enthusiasts like yourself as well as experienced instructors. The RYA (Royal Yachting Association) runs a voluntary training scheme for various certificates (see Appendix 5) and you will be able to work towards one of these. Learning from books has its place, but it cannot substitute for professional instruction on the water. Sailing is thankfully free of heavy government interference, and this is largely due to the success of the RYA training scheme, which in turn is due to the support of sailors such as yourself. If the government sees the system working and producing a reasonable level of competence among yachtsmen then hopefully it will leave us alone.

Finding a Berth

When you do get to buying a boat the first thing you must decide is where you will keep and sail her, as these factors may immediately produce a limited shortlist of the types suitable. There are three basic places where you can keep a boat – at home on a trailer; alongside a pontoon in a marina; or out in a harbour on a mooring. The first has the great advantage of costing nothing, but it does entail towing the boat back and forth to the water every time you want to sail, not to mention the business of floating her on and off the trailer each time. It also limits you quite drastically to size and type of boat – little more than 20 feet and of light weight and shallow draft. Such a boat would have little accommodation, and would only be suitable for sheltered estuary and inland waters. If this type of boat suits you, however, there is much to be said for trailing. Not only is it cheap, but it saves you having to antifoul and it eliminates the risk of osmosis (due to the boat not lying in the water for long periods). It also enables you to sail the boat wherever you like without having to make long passages from the home port. There are countless places in the country where such boats can be launched, in-

cluding inland waters. See Appendix 3. The techniques of trailing are discussed at the end of this chapter.

In contrast, a marina berth is generally rather expensive, if you can get one in your chosen marina (see Appendix 3). You will, however, get good facilities for your money at most of them, and this can be well worth the expense if you have a long journey from home to the boat. Car parks, clubhouse and showers; repair and engineering facilities, fuel, water and mains electricity in the berth, shops and so on are increasingly available at most marinas these days. See photo 51. Do read the small print though, as some marinas take commission on boat sales (even if they do not sell them), insist that you use their engineers, prevent you doing your own maintenance, and force you to abide by a myriad of other bureaucratic non-senses. A mooring out in the harbour will free you from most restrictions of this type and be much cheaper and more peaceful than a marina, but it will not have the facilities or convenience. See photo 52. They are also often difficult to obtain.

Which particular harbour or marina you choose will depend on a number of factors – the distance you are prepared to travel; the berthing charges; the facilities you want; the type of cruising you envisage doing (estuary, inland water or sea). The books in Appendix 3 will help you in this choice.

Choosing the Boat

There is a bewildering variety of sailing craft available these days and it can be very difficult for a beginner to choose the most suitable for his purposes. However, they can be classified in certain groups

opposite
Photo 51 Although very convenient, marina berths can be crowded, and sometimes quite difficult to manoeuvre in and out of.

Photo 52

and this makes things somewhat easier. In broad terms we can divide the available boats into four types: trailer-sailers; family cruisers; cruiser-racers; motor-sailers. The natures of these types of boat should be fairly self-explanatory, and you can see examples with brief descriptions in photos 53 to 56.

We can also consider four different types of keel: long keel; short keel; twin keel; lifting keel. You can see some examples and descriptions in photos 57 and 58. There is a wide variety of different rigs available, but the most suitable for a beginner is the bermudan sloop, which has one mast, one jib and one triangular (bermudan) mainsail. All the photographs in Chapter 2 are of a bermudan sloop, and it is the most common on small modern cruisers. You can find details of other rigs in Chapter 15. You should be able to sift through the comments on all these types and sort out the most suitable combination.

There is a further type of sailing cruiser that we should mention, and that is the multihull. Twin-hulled craft are called **catamarans** and triple-hulled craft **trimarans**, the former being more common for cruising and the latter for racing. See photo 59. Although both types are very much faster than single hulled boats, and are more spacious for a given length, they require rather specialised handling and take up so much room in a marina berth you may be charged double. In my view they are not suitable for beginners, and you should not consider one until you have had some years sailing experience.

Although the size of a boat is likely to be decided by your bank manager, you should bear in mind that anything over about thirty five feet is likely to prove a handful for a family crew to sail. Above this size the gear begins to get heavy for women and children to handle; sails are that much larger and more difficult to control in a breeze; much more skill is required when manoeuvring in tight spaces as the boat is too big to simply

Photo 53 A small cruiser that could be easily towed behind a medium sized car. With her shallow draft and limited accommodation, she would only really be suitable for weekend sailing in sheltered waters (*Yachting World*).

Photo 54 A comfortable and seaworthy sailing cruiser suitable for extended family cruising and offshore passage-making in reasonable weather.

Photo 55 A faster and less comfortable type of boat that would sail well in local offshore races.

Photo 56 A small but comfortable motor-sailer. Spacious for her size and with a fairly powerful engine, she would not sail all that well. Motor-sailers vary from motorboat with sails through to sailing boat with motor, and it is difficult to get a really good, seamanlike compromise under about forty feet, due mainly to the windage of the doghouse.

Photo 57 A short-keeled boat turns more easily and rapidly than does one with a long keel. This makes it more manoeuvrable in confined spaces but less directionally stable at sea, especially when running downwind in waves. A very short-keeled boat can be almost impossible to steer downwind in big waves without constantly broaching. The shorter keel reduces wetted surface and thus increases speed, but for cruising the loss of seaworthiness is a heavy price to pay.

Photo 58 Twin keels enable a boat to dry out upright without having to lean against a wall, but are rarely as efficient as a single deep keel when sailing to windward, due to their generally shallower draft and the increased drag (see photo 5). Lifting keels, that can be raised in shallow water and when drying out, are an efficient compromise (as the photo shows), but can suffer from problems due to their extra complexity (*Yachting World*).

Photo 59

push around by hand. Running costs also begin to rise noticeably.

The most commonly used materials for building boats are fibreglass; steel; aluminium and wood. They all have their merits, but fibreglass is undoubtedly the most suitable for a beginner, being the most easily maintained, the most widely available, and the most readily resold. It is important to consider this last point as you may very well, after a couple of seasons sailing, develop a clearer idea of what you want and thus decide to sell and buy something different. A fibreglass boat of a popular make will not only be certain of providing you with a reliable and safe boat now, but will also be easy to sell.

I would suggest that you begin the selection process with a fibreglass monohull family cruiser under thirty five feet, with a long keel, sloop rig, and diesel inboard engine, of a well-known popular class; then deviate from there as your requirements dictate.

Buying the Boat

Having finally decided on the boat you want, it remains only to find a suitable example and buy her. There are many ways of doing this but I would strongly recommend that, as an inexperienced beginner, you buy one through a reputable and well-established yacht broker. You will pay rather more than if you buy privately, but are far less likely to be sold a dud; a good broker has his reputation to consider. Tell him the sort of boat you want and ask him to supply you with details of anything that comes up. Like an estate agent, he will probably shower you with dozens of quite unsuitable boats, but somewhere in amongst them may well be the one you want. Bear in mind that the asking price will be a good deal higher than the expected one!

Having found a likely contender, I would suggest that you first go and have a quiet look at her on your own (or better, with a knowledgeable friend) if she is not too far away. Obviously you will not be able to go aboard and have a good root round, but you will be spared the patter and pressure of the salesman hanging over your shoulder, and you will be able to glean a fair impression of her general condition and a good idea of whether you like her or not. If you are instantly re-pulsed, you can go straight home and save everyone a lot of time and trouble. Human nature being what it is, the less of the broker's time you take up with totally unsuitable boats, the more attention he will be inclined to give you when a decent one turns up.

If you like her, have a good general look over her. Does she seem well cared for, or tatty and run-down? Is the paint peeling or the gelcoat cracked or crazed? If she does not impress you, go home and wait for the next one. If she does, then ring the broker and tell him you are interested, and make an appointment to view with either him or the owner on hand.

Do not attempt to survey the boat in detail, but simply try to decide whether she fits the purpose you have in mind, and gain a general impression of the quality of construction and maintenance. If the internal joinery and fittings look sturdy and well-finished, then the hull probably is also. If the engine compartment is clean and obviously cared for, then the engine is probably well maintained too. If the sails and rigging are stowed neatly and tidily then the owner very likely is a good seaman who looks after his boat. All these are good signs. If you like what you see then go home and think about her. Do not bother with a trial sail at this stage unless you have an experienced friend with you; ten minutes round the harbour will tell you very little about the boat.

If on reflection you are still enthusiastic then get hold of a reputable marine sur-veyor and arrange for him to make a 'preliminary inspection' of the boat in your presence. This will be much cheaper than a full survey, but will be sufficient to show up any serious problems and help you decide whether to proceed with the expense of a full structural survey. If you can arrange a short sea trial with the surveyor then do so; it may not tell you much about the boat but it should tell him a lot. If all goes well with this inspection then you should go ahead with a full survey. There is a good chance that it will show enough minor defects for you to knock the price down by the cost of the survey. If all goes well with the full survey you can haggle a price with the broker, then tell him to proceed with the sale. He should arrange all the paperwork, insur-ance, finance and so on for you, and before long you will be the proud and happy owner of a very suitable boat.

Trailing a Boat

Perhaps the first thing to appreciate is that when a boat is sat on a trailer her full weight must be taken on the keel; there must be no pressure on the hull from the side chocks, which are there merely to hold her steady. If any weight comes on these they will likely be pushed right up through the hull the first time you go over a big bump. The weight of the boat should also be slightly towards the front of the trailer, such that it takes just a bit of effort to lift it onto the towing hitch of the car. This ensures that the back wheels of the car stay on the ground. Too much weight forward, however, could lift the front wheels and make the steering excessively light, perhaps dangerously so. It may seem obvious to say that the overall weight of boat and gear must not exceed that for which the trailer is designed, but it is very easy to pile on extra equipment without realising how heavy it all is. Broken suspension could be the result.

The boat must be lashed down ex-tremely securely, not just to stop her falling off, but also to prevent her shifting fore and aft, and thus upsetting the towing balance. Lashings, be they rope or pro-prietary webbing straps, must exert their pulls fore and aft as well as downwards. Rope lashings should be bowsed down as tightly as possible with waggoner's hitches (see Chapter 6), and they should be terylene rather than nylon, as the latter stretches too much. Protect coamings and gunwhales etc with old carpet or similar where the lashings pass over them. If an outboard motor hangs on the stern, the propeller must be padded and enclosed in a bright orange bag, to both warn and protect passing pedestrians. A proper lighting board should be firmly attached at the stern, showing reflectors, rear lights, brake lights and indicators, as well as the car licence number.

To launch the boat, remove all fastenings, light boards etc and insert the drain bung if one has been removed. Secure a long warp to the bow and have someone hold this while you back the trailer into the water until the boat floats off. If possible haul her alongside a jetty for boarding while you put away the car and trailer. If the tide is ebbing make sure she does not ground, or that could be the end of your day's sailing.

To retrieve the boat, back the trailer into the water until it is deep enough for the boat to float on, then haul her in over the trailer. Gradually tow the trailer clear of the water, at the same time checking that the boat is in the correct position – keel on the keel support and bow in the right place for towing on the road. Marks on the trailer to align with marks on the boat will make this task much easier. Then secure the bow rope to the trailer and tow her clear of the slipway before preparing for the road, so others can use it. Before you go home, wash the boat thoroughly with fresh water, and flush fresh water through engine cooling systems to prevent residual salt corroding the insides. Unless the trailer has special sealed wheel bearings, these should be stripped, cleaned and regreased after each immersion, to avoid inevitable salt water corrosion.

Manoeuvring the trailer backwards – round corners and through gateways –

requires a certain technique. The secret is to forget the car and think only of the trailer and the direction in which you want to swing it (see figure 89). If you want to swing the trailer round in the direction of arrow number one, you need to push the front of it in the direction of arrow number two. Do this by swinging the car as shown by the curved arrow number three. This must not be overdone, however, or you will jack-knife. As the trailer swings towards the desired direction you must reverse the lock on the car's steering so as to follow the trailer round (see figure 90). The trailer can then

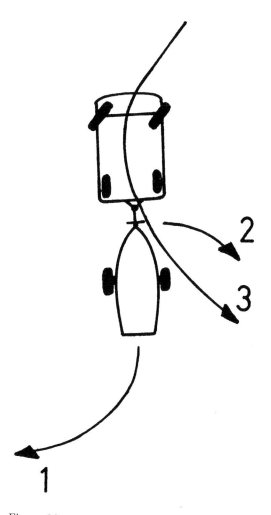

Figure 89

Figure 90

be guided by using the car's steering to swing the front of it in the required direction. With a bit of practice you will soon get the hang of it. Do keep an eye on where the front of the car is going if space is limited.

Towing on the road is fairly straight-forward, as long as you remember that acceleration and braking will both be reduced noticeably in their effectiveness due to the weight of the boat and trailer, and that wide sweeps must be made round corners to prevent the trailer cutting across the pavement. Remember also that when you try to dodge out of a side turning through a gap in heavy traffic, not only will your acceleration be reduced, but also the cars coming along the main road – not seeing your trailer – will fail to appreciate your overall length. Similar problems apply to overtaking. There are a number of specific regulations applying to the towing of trailers, and your local police station should be able to advise you. Do not forget an inflated spare wheel for the trailer.

15

More Advanced Cruising

It is a great mistake when learning a new subject to try and assimilate any inessential material in the early stages. The simpler you can keep things to begin with the better, and I have tried to follow that principle as much as possible throughout this book, introducing new matter only as and when required. The information in this chapter is not necessary for basic coastal cruising, but may be found useful when you have gained some confidence and experience in the basics that have gone before.

Different Sailplans

Although most small sailing cruisers just have the one mast with mainsail and foresail, some larger boats will be found with different **rigs. Ketch** and **schooner** rigs are simply different ways of splitting the sails into smaller, more easily handled sizes on two masts, the ketch (with the shorter mast aft) being the one you are most likely to come across as it is the best compromise between splitting the sails into smaller parts and maintaining an efficient sailing performance to windward. The single-masted boat – called a **sloop** – is the most efficient at beating; the schooner is least efficient. A **yawl** is similar to a ketch but it has a much

smaller **mizzen mast** set further aft, which is really there only to enable a type of jib to be set from it, known as a **mizzen staysail**. It is unlikely that a yawl will sail properly with just jib and mizzen set, whereas a ketch with a decent-sized mizzen will sail and balance well under this combination, and in very strong winds can be reefed simply by handing the mainsail completely. Removing a large sail in the middle of the boat will have little effect on the CE of the sailplan. See figure 16 in Chapter 2. Ketch rig is quite common on modern cruisers over about 35 feet, and has much to recommend it on boats of that size. See photo 60.

Junk rig and **Cat** rig are fairly recent innovations for small cruising yachts, although they have been used on working boats for countless years. The major benefit of junk rig is its simplicity and ease of handling. There is only one sail on the mast, with battens extending from luff to leech. The sail is a simple flat piece of cloth with no complex shape built into it as with conventional sails, and the shape is created by tensioning the battens. Because there are few stresses involved in setting the sail, no standing rigging is required for the mast. It is very efficient downwind but not quite so good to wind-

ward as bermudan rig. It can be hoisted, lowered, reefed and unreefed with great ease by one man controlling lines from the cockpit, and when eased off the battens cause it to lie quietly without the flogging that occurs with conventional sails. For the beginner, however, it has one huge disadvantage: the lack of flapping makes it very difficult to judge when the sail is trimmed properly. For this reason alone I would not recommend it. See photo 61.

Cat rig is basically a bermudan mainsail without the jib, although many modern versions incorporate a variety of complications designed to increase efficiency. Combined with the fact that manoeuvrability is considerably reduced by not having a jib to play with – for shifting the Centre of Effort and backing to turn the bow – this complexity weighs heavily against it for the beginner. Both Junk and Cat rig can be found rigged as two-masted schooners, which are more manoeuvrable as the **foresail** can be used much like a jib for turning the bow and so on. See them advertised in yachting magazines.

Gaff rig – the traditional rig of working vessels in this country – is making a comeback in small yachts. It is slightly more complex to work with than bermudan rig, but less so than Junk or Cat as it handles in the same basic manner as the bermudan. It usually comes in **cutter** configuration, which is the same as a sloop but with two or more headsails – some usually set outboard from the end of a **bowsprit**. The mainsail is split into two – the main being four-sided with the head secured to a yard known as the **gaff**, and hoisted with two halyards; with a triangular **topsail** hoisted above this. One could fill a book with the raging controversy over the relative merits of gaff and bermudan, but for the small boat skipper with some experience the essential benefits of gaff are that it is both

opposite
Photo 60 *(J. A. Hewes)*

Photo 61 *(Yachting World)*

prettier to look at and more interesting to sail than bermudan. See photo 62.

Handling a Spinnaker

A spinnaker is not tacked to the stemhead like a jib but is controlled by lines from the two bottom corners (both called clews) – the leeward line being a sheet and the windward one a **guy**. A pole from the mast to the guy holds the weather clew out to windward. See figure 91. The sail is set up to suit the angle of the wind by adjusting the guy until the luff of the spinnaker just stops flapping. Minor running adjustments are then made by trimming the sheet in and out to keep the sail filling cleanly, just as you would a jib. The pole is prevented from dipping and rising by lines from the outer end, one upwards to the mast and one down to the deck. The jib can be left set at the same time if it will fill, but usually the spinnaker will work

163

Photo 62

better with the jib handed, as it then has an undisturbed flow of air across it. On the other hand, the jib set in the fore-triangle will stop the spinnaker wrapping itself round the forestay if things go wrong. Depending on how bulbous it is the spinnaker can often be flown as close to the wind as a beam reach, although it can be quite tricky to handle at that angle.

To set the spinnaker you should bring it onto the foredeck in its bag with head and both clews hanging out, then attach halyard, sheet and guy. The halyard should lead from the masthead to leeward of the forestay and then to the head of the sail so that the sail is hoisted out clear to leeward of everything. The sheet goes aft outside all rigging to a block on the quarter and thence to a winch and cleat. The guy should go from the sail round ahead of the forestay then through the end fitting on the pole (the opening part of the fitting being uppermost), then aft outside rigging on the weather side to the quarter as for the sheet. Fix the spinnaker pole to the mast and set it horizontally at a

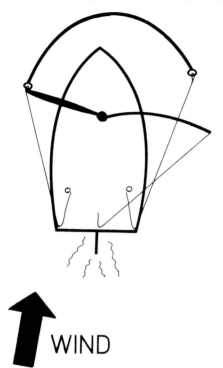

WIND

Figure 91

sheet. Set up the pole topping lift and gybe the mainsail. Trim the spinnaker again, the old sheet now being the guy and vice versa. Keep the spinnaker filling during the gybe or it will wrap itself round the forestay.

Drying Out Alongside

It is sometimes necessary to dry a boat out alongside a wall or jetty to antifoul, scrub or inspect the bottom; or simply because you want to visit a harbour from which the tide retreats completely at Low Water. If you have twin keels this is a simple matter of ensuring that the bottom is smooth and hard (firm sand or shingle), then mooring up and letting her take the ground as the tide goes away. Make sure there is sufficient slack in your mooring warps to let her go right down, if you are alongside a wall. With twin keels this latter restriction is not essential as she can be dried out in the middle of a beach, needing nothing to lean against. If you do this you must moor the boat fore and aft; the simplest way being to let go the kedge anchor astern as you go in, then take a line ashore at an angle from each bow and position her where you want her. The best way to check the suitability of the bottom for drying out is to go and look at it yourself at Low Water. If this is not possible, you will have to settle for local advice; ask the harbourmaster or boatyard manager, not some local leaning on the wall. You can check for large obstructions by dragging a chain along the bottom at the spot you have chosen, and prod about with a long boathook to check the firmness. A wall should be checked for protuberances that could cause bother with the fenders as she goes down. Drag a leadline along it to feel for any. See photo 64.

If you have a single keel, you will need to lean the boat against the wall, and this must be done with some care. The safest way is to list her slightly towards the wall by putting weights on that side of the deck

suitable height (find from experiment), with the downhaul and topping lift. Then haul the spinnaker up as fast as possible; at the same time pulling in on sheet and guy to control and fill it and swing it round ahead of the boat. See photo 63.

To get it down you reverse the process. Slacken guy until the pole swings onto the forestay and the sail is behind the mainsail, then lower steadily, hauling the sheet into the cockpit until you can grab the foot of the sail and haul that into the cockpit. Unclip all lines and stow them, together with the pole, then stuff the sail in its bag foot first, leaving both clews hanging out of the sides ready for the next use. To gybe the spinnaker, haul on the line to the pole end fitting to open it, whereupon the guy will jump out of it. Then lower the topping lift to bring the end of the pole inside the forestay, swing the end round to leeward and clip the fitting up over the

Photo 63 (*Yachting World*)

Photo 64 These boats are dried out against posts, a system commonly found in marinas with sufficient tidal range to allow drying out in a shallow corner.

– anchors, chain, gas bottles, dinghy half filled with water. She must list just enough to ensure that she leans that way, and no more; excessive list will put a big strain on the hull where it rests against the wall. A safety line can be rigged using a halyard from the masthead to the shore, which should be hauled tight when the boat has grounded; or a sliding line can be rigged from the shore to a large shackle that can slide up and down the inside shroud as she rises and falls. Remember to remove these before you leave! Fenders should be fat, numerous, and set to bear against strong points inside the boat – bulkheads for example – and preferably have a plank of wood suspended between them and the wall, partly to prevent the wall chafing the fenders and partly to ensure that the weight is spread evenly along the fenders should gaps appear lower down the wall.

As the boat goes down you must keep mooring warps tight, and adjust them as required to ensure that she remains close to the wall, to make her dry as near upright as is safe, thus reducing to a minimum the weight on the **topsides**. Boats with short keels must be kept secured tightly at bow and stern to prevent them toppling forward or back, but a long-keeled boat will usually dry out bows down a bit due to the angle of the keel, and the head rope must be slackened a little as she grounds to allow for this. Be very wary of walking anywhere on deck away from where she actually leans against the wall; many modern boats are not very stable when dried out. This instability may prove a problem in some places, where drying out is done against posts rather than a wall, and experienced advice should be taken if in doubt.

Mooring to Two Anchors

In a restricted space you may find insufficient room to swing round a single anchor, in which case you should lay two – one upstream and the other down. With the warps joined and lowered beneath the keel, the boat will swing round this point as though it were a mooring. See figure 92. There are two ways of doing this. One is to let go the first anchor as you approach the berth, then steadily pay out twice the calculated length of cable for the depth as you head slowly through and beyond the chosen spot. Then let go the other anchor and veer its cable at the same time as hauling in the other one, until both anchors have out the correct length of cable for the depth. Lash the two warps together very firmly and lower the join down below the keel so the boat can swing without fouling them. The main

anchor and warp should be laid in the direction to hold you against the strongest strain – usually the ebb tide. This procedure is known as a **Running Moor.**

The other method, known as a **Dropping Moor**, is to go past the berth then let go the first anchor and drop back until twice the calculated length is out. Then let go the other anchor and haul back, veering the second warp, until they are middled. It is usually easiest to let go the lighter warp first as this is the one that has to be hauled half back in again! Weighing the anchors is the reverse process – one warp has to be veered sufficiently to get the boat over the other anchor to weigh it, before hauling back to weigh the first. Again, you will find it easier to veer the light one if possible.

Cruising Offshore

When you have gained some confidence and experience you will undoubtedly get itchy feet to be off to distant exotic

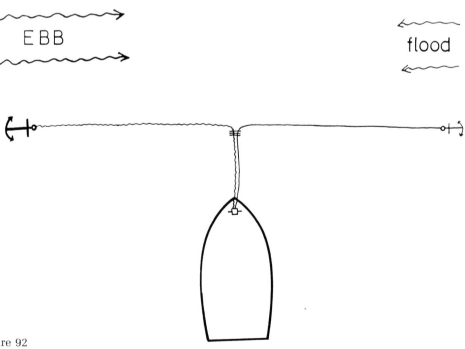

Figure 92

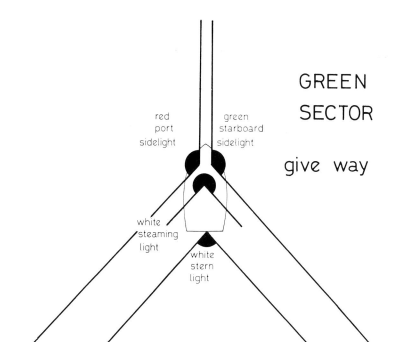

red
port
sidelight

green
starboard
sidelight

GREEN
SECTOR

give way

white
steaming
light

white
stern
light

OVERTAKING
SECTOR

harbours. The information in this book will cover you for most eventualities, but more study of navigation will be advisable, to go with the practice and experience you should have accumulated before attempting a long passage. Much useful information will be found in the Almanac on such matters as Customs Regulations, the flying of courtesy ensigns in foreign harbours and so on, as well as a nautical glossary in most continental languages.

It is important to appreciate, however, that a long passage is much more than just a longer short passage. The weather must be studied and understood with particular care as the risk of being caught in bad weather is that much greater. The boat and her crew must be in excellent condition, able to withstand any conditions at sea, as you may not have time to get safely

Figure 93 These are the lights that small powerboats, and sailing craft under power, should carry. You can see the sectors over which they shine. The steaming light should be higher than the others, perhaps halfway up the mast. It is not exhibited when sailing. When under sail, besides stern and side lights, you may also carry a red light above a green light at the masthead, both showing all round 360°. Many small boats these days have a tricolour lantern at the masthead, incorporating both sidelights and sternlight in one unit, using only one bulb, which saves a lot of drain on the battery. For Rule of the Road purposes overtaking vessels are those within the arc of the sternlight; and you should give way – when under power – to vessels in the sector of your starboard sidelight, if possible by altering to starboard and passing astern of them.

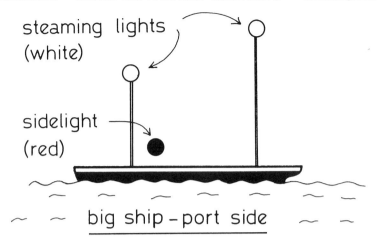

steaming lights
(white)

sidelight
(red)

~ ~ big ship – port side ~ ~

Figure 94 It should be apparent that if this ship alters course – towards or away from you – his two steaming lights will draw closer together. If he is pointing right at you, the after one will be directly above the for'ard one, and the movement of the for'ard one will then indicate the way his bow is swinging. With a little thought and experience, you should be able to work out most of the time what a big ship is doing from the movement and proximity of his two steaming lights.

into shelter if a storm brews up or fog comes down. It can be very tiring at sea on a long passage, so you must institute a system of **watches**, whereby a regular routine of steering, keeping lookout, cooking, resting and so on is imposed on the crew. You cannot just muddle along with everyone hanging about, or when something happens you will all be too tired to cope.

Sufficient food, water, fuel and gas should be on board to last at least twice the expected passage time, partly to allow for delays and partly in case you cannot replenish them at the first port of call. The Almanac and Pilot will contain advice on the facilities you can expect to find in a port, but they might be out of date by the time you get there.

Sailing at night is not difficult but it does take getting used to, and it can be very cold and tiring. Navigation lights must be carried (see figure 93) so that other shipping can both see and identify you. When you cannot see clearly you will find it difficult to check whether a ship is on a collision course by lining it up with a stanchion or shroud (see Chapter 4) and you should take a series of bearings of it with the hand-bearing compass. If the bearings remain steady over a period of time then the ship is converging on you. See Chapter 4 and Appendix 4 for information on Rule of the Road. In practice it is usually wise to alter course to avoid big ships, as they may not see you, even on radar. But do so in good time, or you may find him altering as well, thus causing much confusion and possible danger. If the bearing draws steadily ahead, he will pass ahead; if it draws steadily astern, that is where he will go. You can tell immediately if he alters course, by watching the movement of his two steaming lights. See figure 94.

An offshore passage to a foreign port is an exciting venture. Knowledge, experience, preparation and caution will all help to make it a calm and safe one. Think of all the things that could possibly go wrong, and prepare for them. You should then enjoy your sailing. I hope this book will get you off to a good start.

Appendices

1 *EQUIPMENT LISTS*

Inland and Sheltered Waters

Main anchor and warp
Mooring warps (4 long ones minimum)
Lifebelts (one with light)
Fire extinguishers
Torches (2 powerful ones)
Boarding ladder
Fenders
Boathook
Bucket on lanyard
Local tide table
Warm clothes, and a change
Normal domestic items for galley etc
Kedge anchor and warp
Bilge pumps (one manual)
First aid kit and manual
Fire blanket
Foghorn
Anchor light
Chain (to secure to mooring buoys)
Deck scrubber
Wooden plank with lines (for berthing on piles)
Local chart
Buoyancy aids
Harnesses for small children
Waterproofs

Coastal and Open Waters

All the above plus the following:
Navigation lights
Safety harnesses
Dinghy (and liferaft?)
Pair of dinghy crutches and spare
Anchor and warp for dinghy
Pair of dinghy oars and spare
Baler for dinghy
Pump and repair kit (inflatable dinghy)
Radar reflector
Flares (red hand; red parachute; white hand)
Steering compass
Log (trailing or hull-mounted)
Echo-sounder and/or leadline
Nautical almanac
Parallel ruler
Pencils (half a dozen 2B)
Pencil sharpener
Navigator's notebook
Metmaps (or similar)
Barometer
Binoculars (7×50)
Hand-bearing compass
Charts of complete areas and harbours
Pilot book of complete area
Dividers (single-handed type)

Rubber
Pair of compasses
Logbook
Radio with long wave (for shipping fore-
  casts)
Clock or watch (quartz for accuracy)

Spares and Repairs

Batteries (torches etc)
Bulbs (lights and torches)
Diaphragm and valves (bilge pump)
Oil (engine, gearbox and reduction box)
Distilled water (main batteries)
Fuel and oil filters
Raw water pump impeller (if Jabsco type)
Injectors and fuel lines for diesel engines
Sheer pins and starter cord for outboard
  engines
Plugs, points, condenser, distributor cap
  and HT leads (petrol)
Thermostat
Impellers (power bilge pumps)
Drive belts (generator, water pump)
Emergency tiller
Grease for stern gland
Vaseline for battery terminals
Freeing oil
Strong waterproof tape to repair hoses
Hermetite jointing compound for gaskets
Gasket material
Hoses
Bulldog grips for joining wires
Battery jump leads
Fuses for all equipment and switchboard
Foghorn canister (for aerosol type)
Waterproof spray
Insulating tape for electrical repairs
PTFE tape for plumbing repairs
Stern gland packing

Hose clips
Emery boards and abrasive paper
Clean rags
Hand cleanser

Tools and Equipment

Spanners to fit all nuts on boat
Water pump spanner
Adjustable spanner
Small chain wrench to remove filters
Small crowbar
Hacksaw and spare blades
Vice to clamp to bench or table
Sharp knife and marlinspike (in holster to
  carry with you)
Oilstone to sharpen blades
Hydrometer to check batteries
Gas bottle spanner for gas stoves
Bits of electrical wire
Ball of terylene string
Nuts, bolts, screws etc
Stillson wrench
Mole grips
Pliers (stub and long-nosed)
Screwdrivers (selection)
Claw hammer
Files
Wire brush
Feeler gauge for checking clearances
Primus prickers (for primus stoves and
  heaters)
Sparkplug spanner (petrol engines)
Seizing wire
Odd lengths of rope
Sail repair kit
Selection of shackles
Boltcroppers (very useful if mast goes
  overboard)

2   *ELECTRONIC EQUIPMENT*

This is no more than a brief survey of popular equipment available and its uses. For full details see the Almanac and the relevant book in Appendix 3. Much information on electronic and other equipment can be gleaned from yachting magazine advertisements and tests, and there is a great deal of it about; some useful, some useless, some no more than expensive toys, and none essential for small boat coastal sailing.

Radio-telephone

There are two types in common use – VHF and MF. The latter is bulky, complicated to use, very expensive and has a long range; it is not necessary for coastal sailing. VHF is small, cheap and very simple to operate, with sufficient range for coastal work. It is a most useful device to have on board. Hand-held portable sets are also available.

Although often touted as a 'safety aid' for making distress calls, VHF has far wider-ranging uses than this. Many different channels are available, most for specific purposes such as calling harbour control stations to arrange berthing etc, coast radio stations for weather forecasts, 'link calls' to the shore telephone system, coastguards for weather conditions etc, other ships to check their movements, and so on. It is not simply a handy 'ship's telephone' for idle chatter, but a professional marine communication system that must be used properly, according to certain procedures. Both ship and operator must be licensed for the use of one. Channel 16 is the **Distress and Calling Frequency** – for distress signals and making initial contact before changing to a working frequency – and the set should be tuned to this at all times when not in use. You can see a typical small VHF set in photo 65.

Photo 65 A typical small VHF radiotelephone commonly found on small yachts. It has all the channels you could possibly want, and can scan back and forth between a selected channel and channel 16, listening in effect to both at the same time.

Radar

This device can detect objects (ships, buoys, coastline etc) and display them as blobs of light on a screen rather like a small TV set. Although rarely found on small sailing cruisers because of their bulk and the windage of the aerial, they get smaller and lighter every year, and so do the boats that fit them. In capable hands radar can be invaluable in the dark and in poor visibility, for both navigation and collision avoidance, but it requires skill and experience to tune and interpret the picture properly. It works by bouncing radio signals off objects and detecting the echoes, which vary in strength considerably depending on the shape and composition of the object. Good echoes come

Photo 66 A small boat radar scanner. The windage is considerable, and these are not very practical for boats much under forty feet. Modern displays are rather like small colour television sets and can do all sorts of useful things like sound an alarm on detecting a ship within a certain range, and so on.

from big steel ships, high cliffs, tall harbour walls and so on. Weak or non-existent echoes are obtained from low coastlines, small, wooden or fibreglass boats, buoys without radar reflectors and so on. Waves return echoes which can hide those from small boats, and it is important to understand what the radar operator on a big ship may or may not see on his screen, even if you do not have radar yourself. You can see a typical small boat set in photo 66.

Radio Direction Finder (RDF)

This gadget enables you to take compass bearings of certain radio stations marked on the chart, with which a fix can be constructed just as from visual bearings. It is very useful in poor visibility, but has many limitations that must be clearly understood. Generally it is inaccurate and unreliable at very short ranges; at ranges above the quoted maximum for the transmitting station; at night; and when the signal crosses land at any angle other than 90°. It is also much affected by magnetic and electrical influences on the boat, and needs to be installed and calibrated properly. It is cheaper but nowhere near as useful as the following electronic navigators.

Decca Navigator

This is a magic box that gives a continuous readout of your latitude and longitude to an accuracy of about 200 yards. For many years it has been in use on virtually every commercial vessel in European waters, and is now produced in small and cheap enough form to be in use on huge numbers of pleasure cruisers too. It works by measuring differences between special radio waves received from transmitters dotted about Britain and Europe, and is generally considered to be extremely reliable, even telling you itself if it is receiving an inaccurate signal (which it may in certain places). It can also show your speed over the ground, the course to steer to a particular point; the time it will take you and all sorts of other useful things. There are various types and a typical one is shown in photo 67.

Satellite Navigator (Satnav)

This is a similar device to Decca except that it fixes your position from passing satellites. As these only pass over about once an hour at present, it then calculates your position by Dead Reckoning until the next satellite fix. Thus it is not as accurate as Decca, and is more complex to operate as course and speed must be fed into it so it can calculate DR positions between

Photo 67 A small boat Decca Navigator. There are various types of these, ranging from the basic to the sophisticated, but all give a continuous and very accurate readout of the vessel's position in Latitude and Longitude. The more sophisticated ones can calculate course to steer to a turning point (known as a waypoint), mark the position of a man overboard and many other things.

fixes. It does, however, cover the whole world, while Decca covers only Northern Europe. It is roughly the same price as Decca, and may be a more serious contender when a new system comes out eventually giving far more frequent fixes.

Autopilot

This will steer the boat for you as long as it is supplied with electricity. It will not get tired, seasick or fed up. It will not eat or drink anything, it will not argue with you and it will not get drunk every time you go into harbour. On the other hand, it will not keep a lookout, it will not tell you if the weather changes, and it will not turn round and pick you up if you fall overboard. It is very useful on long passages, but do not make the mistake of thinking that it will replace a crew member. There are two basic types – one steers a compass course, and the other keeps the boat at a set angle to the wind. Some can be adjusted to do either. See the magazine adverts.

Wind Indicators etc

There are masses of these instruments on the market – wind speed and direction indicators; boat speed and course indicators and what-have-you. They can usually be connected up into a bank and interfaced with computers and satnavs and all sorts of things. They are useful for racing, when fractions of a minute may matter, but the cruising man should have no need of them. Much of the pleasure and satisfaction of sailing comes from learning to judge these things for yourself simply by watching the boat.

3 SOURCES OF INFORMATION

Main Reference Books

Makers' Manuals for all equipment on board

Nautical Almanac (Reeds or MacMillans) – with information on:

Collision regulations
Fog Signals
Communication systems (radio, flags, lights etc)
Weather forecasting
Navigation light characteristics
Coastguard stations
Distress signals
Tide tables
Harbour information
First aid
Lights and shapes shown by vessels
Manoeuvring signals
Basic chart symbols
Electronic navigation aids
Rescue organisations
Basic coastal navigation
Tidal stream atlases
Pilot books and chart lists
Glossary of nautical terms and much, much else of use and interest

Engineering

The Care and Repair of Marine Petrol Engines – Loris Goring (Adlard Coles 1987)

The Care and Repair of Small Marine Diesels – Chris Thompson (Adlard Coles 1987)

The Outboard Motor Handbook – Nigel Warren (Stanford Maritime 1977)

Boat Electrics – John Watney (David & Charles 1984)

Electronics Afloat - Dag Pike (Nautical 1987)

Maintenance

The Care and Repair of Glassfibre Yachts
– Tony Staton-Bevan (Adlard Coles 1986)

The Care and Repair Below Decks – Percy Blandford (Adlard Coles 1980)

Boat Maintenance – David Derrick (David & Charles 1980)

Navigation

Practical Yacht Navigator – Kenneth Wilkes (Nautical 1987)

Inshore Navigation – Tom Cunliffe (Fernhurst 1987)

Weather

The Yachtsman's Weather Guide – Ingrid Holford (Airlife 1988)

Instant Weather Forecasting – Alan Watts (Adlard Coles 1985)

Medical

The Yachtsman's Doctor – Dr Richard Counter (Nautical 1986)

Sails and Rigging

Modern Rope Seamanship – Colin Jarman and Bill Beavis (Adlard Coles 1985)

The Care and Repair of Sails – Jeremy Howard-Williams (Adlard Coles 1976)

Rigging – Enrico Sala (Adlard Coles 1988)

Easier Rigs for Safer Cruising – John Campbell (Hollis & Carter 1984)

Electrolytic Corrosion

Metal Corrosion in Boats – Nigel Warren (Adlard Coles 1980)

M. G. Duff & Partners: Birdham, Chichester, West Sussex PO20 7EW

Sailing Cruisers

Popular Sailing Cruisers – Charles Smith

(Charles Smith & RYA 1988)

Book of Yachts 1988 – J. Spencer-Smith (Ringwood 1988)

Book of Class Yachts 1962–1987 – J. Spencer-Smith (Ringwood 1988)

Getting Afloat

Where to Launch Your Boat – Diana Goatcher (Barnacle Marine 1988)

Marina and Harbour Guide – (Dawes Publishing 1988)

Britain and Holland Marina Guide – (Sells Publications 1988)

Magazines

Yachting World
Yachting Monthly
Practical Boat Owner

The books etc that I list here are all ones that I would recommend for further study of the subjects listed. There are, of course, many others on these topics and undoubtedly more will have been published since this list was compiled, but these should provide you with a starting point.

Many authors are good on certain aspects of their subjects and not so good on others, and similar books will cover different sections of the same subject. For wide experience you should browse through libraries and nautical bookshops. The major nautical publishers are: *David & Charles; Adlard Coles; Stanford Maritime; Nautical; Barnacle Press; Hollis & Carter;* but many other publishers produce a few. I would also suggest that you read some cruising stories, of which there are a great many available from a wide variety of publishers.

Magazines are a most useful source of information on all topics, particularly tests of new boats, prices and details of secondhand boats, current equipment reviews and adverts, as well as many expert articles on all manner of seamanship and navigation topics etc. The above three are issued monthly. *Yachting World* is general and very wide-ranging in its coverage of sailing topics. *Yachting Monthly* specialises in cruising material. *Practical Boat Owner* is chock full of practical information, especially for the small boat DIY man.

4   USEFUL REFERENCES

Communications

Phonetic Alphabet and Morse Code
A   ALPHA   · —
B   BRAVO   — · · ·
C   CHARLIE   — · — ·
D   DELTA   — · ·
E   ECHO   ·
F   FOXTROT   · · — ·
G   GOLF   — — ·
H   HOTEL   · · · ·
I   INDIA   · ·
J   JULIET   · — — —
K   KILO   — · —
L   LIMA   · — · ·
M   MIKE   — —
N   NOVEMBER   — ·
O   OSCAR   — — —
P   PAPA   · — — ·
Q   QUEBEC   — — · —
R   ROMEO   · — ·
S   SIERRA   · · ·
T   TANGO   —
U   UNIFORM   · · —
V   VICTOR   · · · —
W   WHISKY   · — —
X   X-RAY   — · · —
Y   YANKEE   — · — —
Z   ZULU   — — · ·

Use these words to spell out callsigns and difficult or foreign words.

R/T Distress Procedure
Tune set to Distress Frequency – VHF = Channel 16; MF = 2182 kHz Transmit following Distress Call on High Power:
  – 'MAYDAY MAYDAY MAYDAY this is (boat's name 3 times)'
  – 'MAYDAY this is (boat's name)'
Transmit Distress Message:
  – position of boat (bearing and distance from landmark is best)
  – nature of emergency (sinking; on fire; etc)
  – type of assistance needed (pumps; firefighting; rescue of crew)

  – number of persons on board (so all can be accounted for after)
  – any other useful information (rate and direction of drift etc)
Listen for a reply. Repeat complete call until reply heard.

For problems less than grave emergency substitute for the word MAYDAY:
PAN-PAN   =urgent message concerning safety of crew or ship
              – (request medical advice etc)
SAYCURITAY =important message concerning navigation or weather danger
              – (report floating wreckage and suchlike)

Keep set tuned to Distress Frequency when not in use.
Teach all crew members to send Distress Call.
Fix details of procedure next to radio.

Important Signals

International Code – Single Letter Signals
A   I have a diver down – keep clear
B   I am loading, unloading or carrying dangerous cargo
C   Yes; affirmative
D★ Keep clear of me, I am manoeuvring with difficulty
E★ I am altering course to starboard
F   I am disabled – communicate with me
G   I require a pilot – OR – I am hauling nets
H★ I have a pilot on board
I★ I am altering course to port
J   I am on fire with dangerous cargo – keep clear
K   I wish to communicate with you
L   You should stop your vessel instantly

M My vessel is stopped and making no way
N No; negative
O Man overboard
P Vessel is about to sail – OR – my nets are caught on the bottom
Q My vessel is healthy and I require free pratique
R★ – (no meaning except by sound in fog – see *Fog Signals*) –
S★ My engines are going astern
T★ Keep clear, I am engaged in pair trawling
U You are standing into danger
V I require assistance
W I require medical assistance
X Stop what you are doing and watch for my signals
Y I am dragging my anchor
Z I require a tug – OR – I am shooting nets

Use International code flag; or morse code light; or morse code sound.
★ = use sound only as *Fog Signal* or *Manoeuvring Signal* (see below).

Distress Signals
1 Gun or explosive signal fired about once a minute
2 Continuous sounding of foghorn
3 Red flares – rocket, parachute or hand
4 Orange smoke signal (hand flare or floating canister)
5 Flames on the vessel (rag on boathook soaked in paraffin)
6 S-O-S sent in morse by any means (usually light or sound)
7 The word MAYDAY on a radio-telephone (see *R/T Distress Procedure*)
8 International code flags – N above C
9 A square flag and a round shape hoisted together
10 Slow, repeated raising and lowering of outstretched arms
11 Built-in alarm signals from radio transmitters
12 Signals from Emergency Position Indicating Radio Beacons (EPIRBS)
13 Ensign hoisted upside down
14 Ensign made fast high in the rigging
15 Article of clothing attached to oar – blowing horizontally

Use only in situation of grave danger; for urgent advice (eg medical) see *International Code* (F, K, V and W) and *R/T Distress Procedure.*

Danger Signals
The following signals (from lightship, coastguard etc) mean:
– 'You are standing into danger'.
Code flag U
Code flags N above F
U in morse by light or sound
Gun or white flare
Rocket sound signal showing white stars
Explosive sound signal repeated
Code flags P above S (by lightship means 'Do not come closer')

Fog Signals
Power vessel under way:
– sounds 1 long blast every 2 minutes
Power vessel stopped:
– sounds 2 long blasts every 2 minutes
Sailing vessel, fishing vessel, a towing vessel, a vessel not under command, or a vessel restricted in manoeuvrability:
– sounds Morse code D (– · ·) every 2 minutes
Vessel being towed (if manned):
– sounds Morse code B (– · · ·) every 2 minutes
– (immediately after tug's signal)
Vessel at anchor:
– 5 seconds ringing of a bell for'ard every 1 minute
– followed by 5 seconds on a gong aft (vessels over 100 metres)
– may sound Morse code R (· – ·) to warn approaching vessel
Vessel aground:
– 3 strokes on bell; then anchor signal; then 3 strokes on bell
Pilot vessels:

– suitable signal from above list
– may also sound Morse code H (· · · ·)
On hearing fog signal ahead – sound yours immediately after

Manoeuvring Signals
I am altering course to STARBOARD
– 1 short blast (·)
I am altering course to PORT
– 2 short blasts (· ·)
My engines are running ASTERN
– 3 short blasts (· · ·)
Are you taking enough avoiding action?
– 5 short blasts (· · · · ·)
I intend to OVERTAKE you:
– 2 long blasts (— —) and:
– on your STARBOARD side
– 1 short blast (— — ·)
– on your PORT side
– 2 short blasts (— — · ·)
I agree to be OVERTAKEN
– Morse code C (— · — ·)
I am approaching a bend in the channel
– 1 long blast (—)
Use only when vessels are in sight of one another.
Short blast = 1 second; Long blast = 5 seconds.
3 short blasts does not imply the vessel is actually moving astern.
Note use of Morse signals with suitable International code meanings.

Rule of the Road

Sailing vessels meeting:
– port tack keeps clear of starboard tack
– windward vessel keeps clear of leeward vessel (on same tack)

Sailing vessels keep clear of:
– vessels they are overtaking
– vessels fishing

– vessels not under command
– vessels restricted in manoeuvrability

Weather Information

Gale Warnings
Imminent – within 6 hours of issue by Met. Office
Soon – 6 to 12 hours after issue
Later – over 12 hours after issue
Warnings are issued some time before broadcast – listen for time.
Warnings broadcast on Radio 4 at next change in programme and after news.
Warnings broadcast by Coast Radio stations on VHF and MF.

Forecast Times
Radio 4: 1500m (200kHz) Long Wave
Shipping Forecast – 0555; 1355; 1750; 0033 (Clock time)
Inshore Forecast – end of day's broadcasting
Land Forecast – 1255; 1755

Visibility in Sea Areas
Good – over 5 nautical miles
Moderate – 2 to 5 nautical miles
Poor – ½ to 2 nautical miles
Fog – less than ½ nautical mile

Speed of Pressure Systems in Forecast
Slowly – less than 15 knots
Steadily – 15 to 25 knots
Rather quickly – 25 to 35 knots
Rapidly – 35 to 45 knots
Very rapidly – over 45 knots

Barometer Changes (rough guide only)
Over 5 mb in 3 hrs – almost certain Force 6
Over 8 mb in 3 hrs – almost certain Force 8

The Beaufort Scale

Force	Approximate Wind Speed (knots)	At Sea	Ashore
0	0	*Calm* No ripples on surface. Any swell is not caused by wind	*Light* Smoke rises vertically
1	2	*Light Air* Patches of ripples on surface	*Light* Smoke drifts. Stirring of flags
2	5	*Light Breeze* Surface covered by ripples and waves up to 12 inches	*Light* Wind can be felt on face, rustles leaves and moves flags
3	5–10	*Gentle Breeze* Small waves, 2-3 feet high, and occasional white horses	*Gentle* Continuous movement of leaves, twigs and flags
4	10–15	*Moderate Breeze* Waves increase to 4-5 feet and white horses are common	*Moderate* Dust and paper blown about. Smaller branches swayed
5	15–20	*Fresh Breeze* Crested waves of 6-8 feet. Spray blown from crests	*Fresh* Small trees sway about. Waves formed on inland waters with crests
6	20–25	*Strong Breeze* Waves of 8-12 feet with spray streaks and crests foaming	*Strong* Large branches swayed. Humming in telephone wires
7	30–35	*Moderate Gale* White foaming crests to waves of 12-16ft, broken away in gusts	*Strong* Large trees swayed. Difficulty in walking against wind
8	35–40	*Gale* Sea rough and disturbed. Waves 20-25 feet, with 'boiling' patches	*Gale* Branches snapped off, small trees blown down. Extreme difficulty in walking against wind
9	40–45	*Severe Gale* Sea covered in white foam, waves 25-30 feet. Visibility reduced by spray	*Gale* Chimneys and slates blown down
10	50–55	*Storm* 30-40 feet waves. Visibility badly affected	*Whole Gale* Large trees uprooted. Buildings damaged or blown down
11	60–65	*Violent Storm* Air full of spray. Large vessels may be damaged by waves of 45 feet	*Storm* Major structural damage
12	65+	*Hurricane* Waves over 45 feet will damage large ships and may cause small craft to founder	*Hurricane* Very severe structural damage

Engine Fault Finding

A Starter will not turn, or turns very slowly

1 Starter battery isolating switch turned off
2 Bad connection between starter motor and battery
3 Battery discharged or with internal fault
4 Bad connection in ignition-switch circuit to solenoid
5 Bad connection inside solenoid
6 Bad connection inside starter motor (probably sticking brushes)
7 Starter motor bendix jammed in fly-wheel

B Starter turns over, but engine does not fire

1 No fuel delivery
2 No air
Diesel
3 Insufficient cranking speed (see Section A)
4 Insufficient or faulty starting aid when engine cold
5 Air in fuel line
Petrol
6 Insufficient choke on cold engine
7 Excessive choke on hot engine
8 Damp ignition electrics (HT)
9 Bad connection in ignition circuit (HT or LT)
10 Faulty or fouled sparkplugs
11 Pitted or incorrectly set points
12 Faulty condenser
13 Cracked distributor cap/HT lead insulation

C Engine runs roughly, labours or stops

1 Erratic air supply
2 Erratic fuel supply (dirt in fuel or air in diesel)
3 Erratic ignition
   faulty injector (*diesel*)
   see Section B: 8–13 (*petrol*)
4 Engine working too hard
   weed or rope round propeller

engine overheated (see Section D)
no oil in engine or gearbox

D Engine overheats

1 Blockage in raw-water circuit
2 Serious leak in either water circuit
3 Thermostat failing to open
4 Faulty raw- or fresh-water pump
   airlock in pump
   broken pump impeller
   slack drive belt/broken shaft
5 Blocked fan filter or air inlet (*air cooled*)
6 Engine working too hard (see Section C: 4)
7 Lack of cooling air in engine room

E Oil pressure drops

1 Serious oil leak
2 Clogged oil filter
3 Dirt jamming oil-pressure relief valve open
4 Water or fuel in the oil

F Generator does not charge

1 Loose drive belt
2 Bad connection in generator circuit
3 Internal fault in battery (engineer to test)
4 Battery-isolating switch off
5 Ignition switch off (*diesel*)
6 Fault in generator (probably sticking brushes; see manual)
7 Fault in regulator (can also cause over-charging; engineer to test)

G Engine will not drive boat

1 Broken shear-pin (*outboard*)
2 Propeller fallen off or seriously damaged (*inboard*)
3 Gearbox clutch slipping
4 Boat is aground!

H Smoke from exhaust

Black
   Faulty injector (excessive fuel) (*diesel*)
   Overloaded engine (*diesel*)
   Over-choked engine (*petrol*)

Too rich fuel/air mixture (excessive fuel) (*petrol*)

White

Faulty injector (insufficient fuel) (*petrol*)

Poor compression (fuel not igniting) (*diesel*)

Weak fuel/air mixture (insufficient fuel) (*petrol*)

Blue

Normal colour due to burning oil (*two-stroke*)

Internal wear (oil burning in cylinders) (*four-stroke*)

Pale Blue

Normal colour of exhaust (*diesel*)

I Noise from engine

Loud screeching front of engine
Slipping drive belt (loose or greasy)
Worn water pump bearings

Regular tapping at top of engine
Valve clearances too great

Light tinkling inside engine
Broke piston ring (compression low in that cylinder)

Dry rattle at high revs
Worn big end bearings (with low oil pressure)

Light rattle front of engine
Loose, worn timing chain

Heavy rumbling, vibration
Worn crankshaft, main bearings

Unusual noises around engine
Loose fittings vibrating

Whining from gearbox
Worn gears or no oil

Rumble, vibration at stern
Propshaft misaligned
Prop damaged
Propshaft bearings, flexible coupling worn

J Engine performs badly

Fails to reach maximum rpm
Prop too coarse a pitch

Fails to drive boat at expected speed (or max revs too high)
Prop too fine a pitch

Lacks power
Low compression (internal wear – see manual; blown head gasket)
Generally out of tune

5   THE RYA TRAINING SCHEME

This is a voluntary system of qualifications for yachtsmen covering dinghy sailing, motor cruising and sail cruising. Full details of the last named may be found in the RYA booklet *Training G15/83*. There are three good reasons why all yachtsmen should strive for certificates under this scheme:

1 It provides a known and accepted level of competence for sailors
2 It discourages the government from interfering in sailing
3 It provides evidence of competence when abroad or chartering

There are five categories of qualification: **Competent Crew; Day Skipper/Watch Leader; Coastal Skipper; Yachtmaster Offshore**; and **Yachtmaster Ocean**, the levels of ability progressing from a useful crew to a skipper capable of taking any boat anywhere in the world. The courses for each category vary, but in general consist of shore-based tuition, practical tuition, and a certain amount of sea time. The first two categories qualify on satisfactory completion of the course, while the three higher grades involve practical and oral examinations. Instruction is given by qualified **Yachtmaster Instructors** and examinations are carried out by **Yachtmaster Examiners**.

Full details of courses, syllabuses and recognised training establishments can be obtained from the RYA at RYA House, Romsey Road, Eastleigh, Hampshire SO5 4Y.

Glossary

Abaft: behind

Abeam: directly out to the side of the boat

A-bracket: fitting to support propshaft outside hull

Adrift: loose; late; broken off

Aft: at the back of the boat

Ahead: forward; in front of the boat

Amidships: in, or in line with middle of boat

Arm the lead: put tallow in lead for sample of seabed

Astern: backwards; reverse; behind the boat

Athwartships: across the boat

Awash: level with the water

Aweigh: anchor is aweigh when just off seabed

Back: wind backs when it shifts anticlockwise

Ballast: weight low down in boat to give stability

Bar: shallow bank across river or harbour entrance

Batten down: secure hatches etc firmly before going to sea

Beam: width of boat at widest part

Bear off: push off from jetty etc

Belay: secure rope round cleat; cancel order

Below: down inside the cabin

Beneaped: stuck aground with tide falling in height to neaps

Bight: loop in rope; middle part of rope

Bilge: inside of boat at very bottom

Binnacle: stand on which a compass is mounted

Bitter end: very end of a rope or chain cable

Boathook: pole with a hook on the end

Bollard: large post for mooring boats to

Bow: front end of a boat

Breastrope: short mooring line straight across to shore

Bring up: come to anchor

Broach: swing violently round broadside to waves

Bulkhead: internal partition wall in boat

Bulwarks: solid wall-like rail around the deck

Buoy: floating sea mark, anchored as guide to navigation

Buoyancy aid: foam-filled waistcoat that helps you float

Cast off: let go of a line or mooring

Cleat: T-shaped fitting to which ropes can be secured

Coaming: raised surround to cockpit etc

Cockpit: well at stern (or amidships) for crew to sit in

Courtesy ensign: small ensign of country being visited

Crown: bottom end of anchor, where flukes begin

Crutch: U-shaped fitting to hold oars when rowing

Deck: flat surface on top of a boat

Deckhead: underneath the deck (inside the cabin)

Dinghy: small open boat, often used as tender for yacht

Displacement: weight of a boat (see Archimedes!)

Draft: depth of boat below waterline

Ebb tide: flows out of harbour and falls in height

Equinoctial tides: very high spring tides occurring near equinoxes

Fairlead: smooth fitting at deck edge to lead ropes ashore

Fair tide: tide that is running with you

Fairway: clear, navigable channel

Fall: loose length of rope leading away from a tackle

Fathom: six feet; little used now charts are metric

Fender: soft plastic sausage to cushion boat against wall

Fetch: distance across water in which waves can build up

Fiddle: rail round cooker etc to stop things sliding off

Fill: a depression fills when it loses energy and fades

Flake: lay rope or chain in loose figure of eight on deck

Flukes: points of anchor that dig in seabed

Flood tide: tide flowing into harbour and rising in height

Fo'c'sle: compartment right forward in boat

For'ard: commonly used contraction of forward

Foul anchor: anchor tangled up in chain or rough seabed

Foul ground: rough seabed unsuitable for anchoring

Foul tide: tide running against you

Freeboard: height of deck above waterline

Galley: kitchen onboard a boat

Gimbals: pivots enabling compass etc to stay upright

Ground tackle: generic term for anchors and warps etc

Guardrail: wire fence around deck edge

Gunwhale: corner between topside and deck (pron: gunnel)

Head rope: mooring line from bow to jetty

Heads: boat's WC

Heaving line: light line with heavy knot on end to throw ashore

Helm: steering position; tiller or wheel

Helmsman: person steering the boat

Holding ground: type and suitability of seabed for anchoring

Inboard: in or on the boat (inboard engine etc)

Isobar: line joining places of equal atmospheric pressure

Jury: makeshift (rudder, rig etc)

Keel: backbone of boat at the bottom; weight under boat

Knot: speed of one nautical mile per hour

Lee shore: shore towards which the wind is blowing

Lee side: the side of boat opposite to the wind

Leeward: away from the wind

Leeway: sideways drift of boat caused by the wind

Lie a-hull: drift with wind and sea with no sail set

Lifejacket: device that will keep unconscious person afloat

Liferaft: special rubber dinghy for abandoning ship

Lighthouse: tall building with guiding light on top

Log: device to measure distance run through water

Logbook: to keep detailed records of a passage

Loom: reflection from clouds of light below the horizon

Lubber's line: fixed line on compass showing boat's heading

Make fast: secure a line to a cleat etc

Marlinspike: tapered steel bar for undoing shackles etc

Millibar: unit of measurement for atmospheric pressure

Mooring: buoy anchored to seabed for tying up to

Mouse: secure pin to shackle with wire to prevent undoing

Nautical mile: about 2000 yards; one minute of latitude

Offing: area of sea away from the shore

Outboard: outside the boat (outboard engine)

Overfalls: steep breaking waves when tides meet

Painter: mooring line permanently attached to dinghy

Pooped: when large wave overtakes boat and breaks over her

Port: left hand side of boat looking forward

Pulpit: strong guardrail round bow

Pushpit: strong guardrail round stern

Quarter: after corner of a boat

Race: rough water caused by fast currents round headland

Reeve: to pass a rope through a block

Riding light: another name for an anchor light

Ringbolt: bolt with large ring attached, for mooring up to

Riser: cable from seabed mooring to buoy on surface

Rowlock: U-shaped gap in gunwhale to rest oar in

Rubbing strake: half-round timber or moulding to protect gunwhale

Rudder: flat plate swivelling at stern to steer boat

Samson post: heavy post on foredeck for anchoring or mooring

Scope: amount of anchor warp in use

Scuppers: large drain holes in bulwarks

Sealegs: you have your sealegs when used to motion of boat

Sea returns: echoes from waves on radar screen

Seizing: secure lashing holding two ropes together

Set: direction in which current or tidal stream runs

Shackle: U-shaped metal fitting closed by screwed pin

Shank: long arm of an anchor

Sheer: to swing about at anchor; curve of boat's deckline

Shoal water: shallow water

Slack water: period of no tidal stream at High and Low Waters

Sounding: depth of water on chart; depth measured by lead

Spring: mooring warp that prevents movement along jetty

Stanchion: post supporting guardrail

Standing part: end of a rope that is secured to something

Starboard: right hand side of boat looking forward

Steerage way: just sufficient speed for the rudder to steer

Stem: the very front edge of the bow

Stern: the back of a boat

Stern rope: mooring line from stern to jetty

Stock: cross piece on anchor making it fall over and dig

Surge: ease warp gradually round cleat when under strain

Swell: long smooth waves left behind after wind dies

Tackle: rope rove through blocks to increase hauling power

Tender: dinghy for getting ashore from boat when anchored

Thwart: athwartship seat in small boat

Tiller: long stick to turn rudder when steering

Topsides: side of boat above waterline

Transducer: underwater sensor for echo-sounder etc

Transom: a flat vertical stern

Trim: fore-and-aft attitude of boat in water

Under way: not attached to the land (not necessarily moving)

Up and down: when anchor cable is vertical

Veer: the wind veers clockwise; to let out cable or warp

Wake: trail of disturbed water left behind moving boat

Warp: general term for mooring ropes, anchor cable etc

Watch: spell of duty for crew – eg steering

Weather shore: shore which the wind is blowing away from

Weather side: side of a boat facing the wind

White horses: waves breaking with white foam

Windage: area of boat above water that wind blows against

Wind-rode: lying to the wind when moored or anchored

Windward: towards the wind

Working end: free end of rope, used to tie knots in

Yaw: to swing from side to side of course being steered

Index

(Page numbers in italics refer to illustrations or captions)

Airstream, *99*
Anchoring, 52, *52*, 53, *56*, 60, 65, 66, 80, 81
  anchorage, *61*, 62–64
  types of anchor, 53, *55*
  buoying the anchor, 64, *64*
  cable, 53, *55*, *56*, 59, 64, *65*, 73–75, 77, 79
  kedge, *55*
  mooring to two anchors, 168, *168*
Anode, 148, *149*
Anticyclone (High), 93, *94*, 97–99, 101
  blocking high, 97
Antifouling, 147
Autopilot, 175

Barometer, 95–97, 101
Beaufort Scale, 93, 181
Bilge pump, 82
Boom vang, 28, *28*, 31, 104, 108
Bowline, 67, *68*, 75
  dipping the eye, 69, *69*
Bowsprit, 163, *164*
Broaching, 107
Buoyancy aid, *79*, 80, 85, 86, *86*
Buoy:
  navigation, 43, *43*, 118, 119, *123, 124*
  mooring, 67, 73–75

Cat rig, 161, 163
Catamaran, 152, *157*
Centre of Effort, 23, *23*, 24, 36, 161, 163
Centre of Lateral Resistance, 23, *23*, 24
Chafe, 67, 73, 75
Charts, 59, *61*, 111–129, *112, 116, 117, 120, 121, 126*
  correcting, 111

measuring distance on, 122
  symbols, 63
Chart Datum, 59, *60, 61*
Clove hitch, 69, *71*
Coastguard, 88, 101
Cockpit dodgers, *10, 11, 14, 16–19, 25, 29*
Compass, *8*, 112, *113*
  adjustment, 113
  bearings, *125, 127*
  handbearing, 112, 113
  rose, 94, *95, 127*, 128
Cruising chute, 37
Cutter, 163, *164*

Decca navigator, 174, *175*
Depression (Low), 93, *94*, 95–97, *96*, 99, *100*, 101
  wave (secondary), 99, *100*
Depth contours, 59, *61*
Deviation, 113, 135
  card, 113, *114*, 135
Dew Point, 98
Dinghy, 77, *78–80*, *79–81*, 85, 88
Distress signals, *87*, 179
Double sheet bend, 70, *71*
Drying height, 59, *60, 61*

Echo-sounder, 60, 112
Electrolysis, *73*, 83, 148, *148*
Engine, 49, 138–145
  fault-finding, 140, 182, 183
  maintenance, 138, 140, 148, 149
  outboard, 79, 81, 83, 85, 138, *139*, 142, *142*
  inboard, 82, 83, 85, 138, *139*
  winter lay-up, 149

manoeuvring, 140–143

Fendering, *25*, 66, 75, 81, 84
Figure of eight knot, 31, *32*
Firefighting, 82, 83, 132
First aid, 84
Fixing, *125*, 128
  departure fix, 128
Flaking cable, 77
Flares, *87*, 88
Fog, 91, 98, 133
  horn, 88, 133
  signals, 179
  precautions, 133
Frapping lines, 34
Fronts (weather), 96, *96*, 97, 99, *100*

Gaff rig, 163, *164*
Gelcoat, 147
Genoa jib, 37
Gooseneck, 26, *26, 27*
Goosewinging, 19, *19–21*
Grounding, 130, 131, *131*
Gybing, 19, *20*, 31, 104, 108
Harness, 87, *87*, 134
Heads, 85
Heave to, 106, *106*
Hull:
  maintenance, 147
  material, 157
  trim, 24

International Code, 178
  danger signals, 179

Junk rig, 161, 163, *163*

Keel, 11, 12, *12, 13*, 23, 39, 153, *156*
Ketch, 161, *162*

Latitude, 119, *120*
Leadline, 60, *62*, 84, 112
Lee helm, 23, 24, 36
Leeway, 12, 39, 40, *40*, 43, 44, 128
Lifebelt, *8, 11, 14, 16–19*, 88, *90*
Lifejacket, 86, *87*
Liferaft, 80, 88
Log (distance), 112
Logbook, 97, 112, *112*
Longitude, 119, *120*

Manoeuvring signals, 180
Man overboard, 107, 133–135, *134*
Marinas, 45, 50, 67, *152*, 153
Metmaps, 101
Mizzen, 161, *162*
  staysail, 161

Mooring, *25*, 28, 46–49, 74, *152*, 153
Mooring lines, *75*, 75–77, 84
  making fast, 29, 67, *68*, 69, *69*, 73
  rafting up, 75
  slip rope, 73
  springs, 75, *75*, 142, *143*
  taking a turn, 76
Morse code, 178
Motor-sailing, 144, *155*

Nautical Almanac, 52, 59, 62, 63, 84, 101, 111–129, 169
Nautical mile, *122*
Navigation lights (boat), *169, 170*

Occlusion, 99, *100*
Offshore passages, 169
Osmosis, 147

Pilot book, 111–129
Preventer, 108
Propellers:
  danger to swimmers, 85
  fouled, 136
  handing of, 140
  paddlewheel effect, 140, *140*

Radar, 88, 173, *174*
  reflector, *30*, 88, *89, 123*
Radio direction finding, 174
Radio-telephone, 84, 125, 129, 135, 173, *173*
  distress procedure, 178
Reefing, 69, 103, 104, *104, 105*
Reef knot, 69, *70*
Rescue procedures, 136, 137
Ridge of high pressure, 99
Riding turn, 72
Roller-furling jib, 28, *30*, 35, 37, 105
Roller-reefing jib, 37, 105
Rolling hitch, 72, *73*
Round turn & 2 half hitches, 67, *68*, 73, 80
Royal Yachting Association, 151, 182
Rule of the Road, 52, *169*, 180

Satellite navigator, 174
Seacocks, 85, 132
Seasickness, 110
Schooner, 161, 163
Shackle, 73, *73*, 74, 147
Sheet bend, 69, *70, 71*
Shipping forecast, 91, 101
Shipping lanes, 133
Sinking, 131, *132*
Sloop, 38, 161, 163
Sounding, 59, *60, 61*
Spinnaker, 37, 163–165, *165, 166*
Storm jib, 37